Weekends
for
wine lovers
IN THE SOUTH ISLAND

about the author

Liz Grant is a Christchurch-based freelance writer with a special interest in the arts and an even stronger interest in wine. Her biggest challenge in writing this guide was fending off all the friends who offered to help with research. However, she had some wonderful weekends in the process and is now full of admiration for the creativity and passion of the winemakers within these pages.

for wine lovers
IN THE SOUTH ISLAND

Liz Grant

NEW
HOLLAND

For Isla and Laura

First published in 2000 by New Holland Publishers (NZ) Ltd
Auckland • Sydney • London • Cape Town

218 Lake Road, Northcote, Auckland, New Zealand
14 Aquatic Drive, Frenchs Forest, NSW 2086, Australia
24 Nutford Place, London W1H 6DQ, United Kingdom
80 McKenzie Street, Cape Town 8001, South Africa

ISBN: 1-877246-30-X

Managing editor: Renée Lang
Project co-ordinator: Amy Palmer

Design: Graeme Leather, Island Bridge
Editor: Jeanette Cook
Maps: Pauline Whimp

Colour reproduction by Colour Symphony Pte Ltd, Singapore
Printed by Times Offset (M) Sdn Bhd, Malaysia

Contents

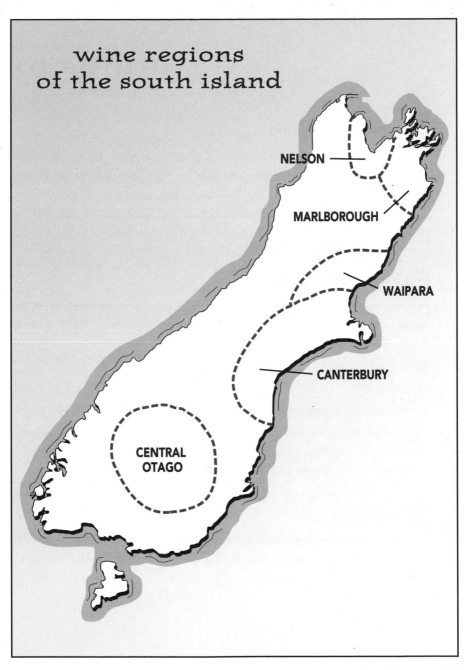

wine regions
of the south island

NELSON

MARLBOROUGH

WAIPARA

CANTERBURY

CENTRAL
OTAGO

guide to

🍴 EATING AND DRINKING

The restaurants and cafés included in this guide have been selected because they are consistently rated highly, and also for their atmospheres, which are relaxed, fun and upbeat. They are generally within easy reach of the wineries and accommodation that we have selected, and are listed in alphabetical order.

🛏 STAYING THE NIGHT

Places to stay have been selected along similar criteria to those used for restaurants, and are also listed in alphabetical order. Each has been given a price code, as follows:

$$$ = $120 to 'the sky's the limit'

$$ = $80-120

$ = rock bottom to mid-range $80

Prices in *Weekends for Wine Lovers* are a guide only and may vary. All prices are based on double/twin share but most cottages and self-contained accommodation can take extra people for an additional cost.

📷 TIME OUT

A selection of summer and winter recreational activities, some of which are unique to the region, and which have been chosen for the most part because of their mainstream appeal.

our guide

WINERIES

All wineries are listed in alphabetical order within their region.

Weekends for Wine Lovers is not intended to be an exhaustive guide to all wineries; its emphasis is on wineries open to the public for tasting, tours and cellar door sales.

Each winery entry includes a list of wines produced:
○   the whites first
●   followed by the reds.

Within these categories they are listed in alphabetical order according to the grape variety (i.e., chardonnay comes before sauvignon blanc and merlot comes before pinot noir). The wines are not listed according to brand, nor according to their status as a premium or everyday quaffing wine. Where a grape variety is not mentioned, the style is listed alphabetically within the list.

MAPS

Please note that the regional maps are not intended to take the place of the more comprehensive road atlas or maps that most of us carry in the car. Their main purpose is to indicate the approximate location of the wineries.

introduction

Welcome to the South Island! Whether you're an overseas visitor or you live in New Zealand, *Weekends for Wine Lovers* will help you make the most of this extraordinary island that has so much to offer. You may have several weekends to spare, or only one, but there is always time to follow exciting wine trails and to take in a few other sights and adventures along the way.

From north to south, the five major wine-producing regions of the South Island are Nelson, Marlborough, Waipara, Canterbury and Central Otago. Their tremendous scenic variety is reflected in the unusual and exciting wines that have emerged over the last couple of decades. Touring the South Island is a wine lover's delight.

The potential for wine production here was slow to be recognised. It may seem astonishing now, but as little as 20 years ago those pioneers among the grapegrowers and winemakers were definitely seen as oddballs! Now the world is exclaiming over Marlborough sauvignon blancs and chardonnays. Montana's Deutz Marlborough Cuvée is a world-beater, and wine lovers rave about Canterbury's chardonnay, Waipara's pinot noir, Central Otago's riesling and pinot noir, and Nelson's riesling and sauvignon blanc. Excellent, spicy gewürztraminer wines and succulent late harvest rieslings are also to be found in many of these regions.

The beautiful landscapes throughout the South Island are an additional bonus. There are the little coves and golden beaches of the northern end of the South Island, in the Marlborough Sounds or across in the Nelson Bays area, where the climate is balmy and the lifestyle relaxed. Meander down to the Blenheim area of Marlborough and you're into the fastest-growing vineyard region in New Zealand. The scenery changes to something quite dramatic with the vines spread across the flood plains of the Wairau Valley or the Awatere Valley, each with a backdrop of hill range upon hill range. Drive to the coastal highway and head south through Kaikoura, enjoying the constant motion of the Pacific Ocean, home to whales, dolphins and seals not far offshore. Turn in once more to the rolling hills of North Canterbury and, later, the flatter reaches of the Canterbury Plains. (The Canterbury area already has two distinct winemaking regions – Canterbury itself and Waipara – but with the expansion of the number of vineyards on Banks Peninsula there could well be a third, clearly defined district in the making.) Enjoy the charming city of Christchurch before heading further south into Central Otago. This is a region of extremes – hot, dry summers and cold, cold winters. But it has long, cool, exceptionally dry autumn weather by New Zealand standards, giving the grapes a long ripening period. It's rocky and craggy, and the vines are grown at high altitude. At Chard Farm in Central Otago New Zealand's first genuine ice wine is produced.

In between your sipping and supping, there's a huge range of activities to indulge in. Depending on your energy level, there is everything from hunting, shooting, fishing, skiing, bungy jumping, river rafting and tramping, to simply wandering around the art galleries, parks and gardens, or picnicking by a river, lolling on a beach or being poled down-river in a punt.

So here's a glass to a wonderful weekend. Or several in a row. Travel safely and, above all, enjoyably.

Liz Grant

nelson

With its fabulous rivers, beaches and lakes, dramatic mountains, lush native bush and sunny climate – not to mention the friendly winemakers and their excellent wines – Nelson can provide enough delights to justify a number of weekend visits.

The region has two main grapegrowing areas – the alluvial Waimea Plains, with their stony soils, and the rolling Moutere Hills, with a heavier clay loam – and each area produces very individual wines. The region is one of New Zealand's sunniest, with long warm summers and cool autumn nights. It already has a reputation for producing delicious, creamy chardonnays. The local Neudorf Moutere Chardonnay is regarded as a classic wine. In recent years some exciting pinot noir and riesling has been coming from the region. And it would be a mistake to overlook the sauvignon blanc and many of the other interesting wines, such as 'Escapade Red' from the Holmes Brothers.

Fruit, tobacco and hops have been the traditional crops of this region and it has long had a good reputation for cider and fruit wines. But in the last 10 years there has been a tremendous expansion in vineyard planting. At the time of writing four new vineyards are about to step onto the stage!

The winemaking trail-blazers of the region were Hermann and Agnes Seifried. They first established themselves in the Upper Moutere district in the mid-1970s and now produce over half the region's wine. Neudorf Vineyards were the next to make a name for themselves. Now Nelson offers one of the most delightful wine trails in the country. Many of the vineyards are open year-round for wine tasting and some also have cafés offering delicious food, much of it locally sourced.

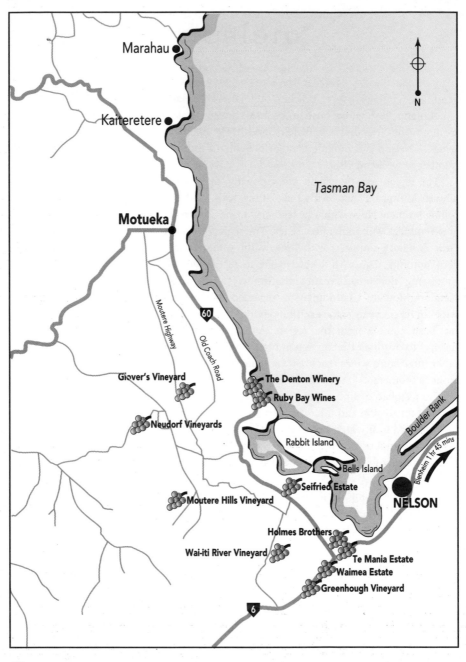

Marahau

Kaiteretere

Tasman Bay

N

Motueka

Moutere Highway

60

Old Coach Road

Glover's Vineyard

The Denton Winery

Ruby Bay Wines

Neudorf Vineyards

Rabbit Island

Bells Island

Boulder Bank

Blenheim 1 hr 45 mins

Seifried Estate

NELSON

Moutere Hills Vineyard

Holmes Brothers

Wai-iti River Vineyard

Te Mania Estate

Waimea Estate

Greenhough Vineyard

6

Wine is high on the list of Nelson's attractions but it isn't the only drawcard. The area has always attracted creative people and it is home to a tremendous number of artists and craftspeople. The city's Bishop Suter Art Gallery is the third-oldest public art museum in the country and some of the finest art of the region can be seen there. One of the added charms of the district is that it's possible to visit many artists in their studios, set in this beautiful countryside. A beautifully produced guidebook, *Art in Its Own Place*, describing 13 cultural trails, is available from local bookshops and the information centre.

To work up an appetite for all these visual delights and taste sensations, the Nelson region offers an extraordinary range of outdoor activities. Two stunningly beautiful, bush clad National Parks are part of the region – Abel Tasman and Kahurangi. Bush walking, camping, sea kayaking, sailing, white water rafting, skiing and snowboarding, horse riding and lolling about on the beach are just some of the outdoor pursuits available in this versatile area. It is no small wonder that it is fast becoming a favourite destination for weekend trips as well as long summer holidays.

 Nelson
Cnr Trafalgar and Halifax Streets
phone (03) 548 2304
fax (03) 546 7393
email: vin@tourism-nelson.co.nz

Motueka
Wallace Street
phone (03) 528 6543
fax (03) 528 6563
email: mzpvin@nzhost.co.nz

Golden Bay
Willow Street, Takaka
phone/fax (03) 525 9136
email: gb.vin@tourism-nelson.co.nz

AUTHOR'S FAVOURITES

Denton Reserve Chardonnay

Neudorf Moutere Chardonnay

Neudorf Moutere Pinot Noir

Richmond Plains Escapade Red

Seifried Sauvignon Blanc

REGIONAL HIGHLIGHT

NELSON ARTS FESTIVAL

The Arts Festival is held at the same time as the Wearable Arts Awards, and these two events create a wonderfully exciting atmosphere in the city just as it's emerging from winter into spring. The arts festival is designed as a showcase for the highly talented local arts community.

For further information, contact the Nelson City Council (03) 546 0200.

the
wineries

The Denton Winery ————————

When Alexandra and Richard Denton and their two children left England in 1991 they hadn't even thought of New Zealand as a place to settle. Calling here on their way to somewhere else, they liked the feel of the country and reconsidered their plans. In 1995 this property came up for sale and thus evolved The Denton Winery. The tasting room and restaurant are on a rise and have a wide verandah looking over an extensive garden and lake. There are also paved and tree-shaded areas to have a light lunch or afternoon tea. Alexandra clearly enjoys this very sociable business and takes pride in offering a simple menu of the best available – award-winning cheeses, local breads and the outstanding local Moutere Gold pickles. Brie and roasted peppers, and blue cheese and spiced figs are just two of the wonderful platters.

Richard had been a home winemaker for a long time and has turned professional with considerable success. An early achievement was the highly rated 1997 pinot noir. The vineyard is small but Richard's aim is to produce distinctive, exquisite wines. He says the soil in the deep, free-draining clay of the Moutere Hills can produce some 'luscious and mouth-filling wines'.

APPELMANS RESTAURANT

294 Queen Street, Richmond
phone (03) 544 0610

Half an hour's drive from Nelson city, this old colonial house is home to an award-winning restaurant. It has an excellent reputation for superb fresh local food. It does have a BYO licence, but also prides itself on its local wine list.

A bonus of the visit is a gallery within the tasting room. Alexandra studied art in England and the gallery displays her striking watercolours.

☞ **Awa Awa Road, Ruby Bay**

Phone/fax: (03) 540 3555

Hours: for tasting and buying wines, same as restaurant.

Eating/other facilities: restaurant open 11am-5pm seven days from Labour Weekend to Easter. Also open some weekends in September/October and in May.

Owners: Richard and Alexandra Denton

Winemaker: Richard Denton

Wines produced

○ Denton Chardonnay, $18-20
Denton Reserve Chardonnay, $24-26
Denton Riesling, $15-17
Denton Sauvignon Blanc, $16-18

● Denton Folly, $35-40
Denton Merlot, $18-20
Denton Nelson Pinot Noir, $18-21
Denton Reserve Pinot Noir, $28-32
Denton Syrah, $24-26

BOAT SHED CAFÉ AND RESTAURANT

350 Wakefield Quay, Nelson
phone (03) 546 9783

The region is famous for its seafood and the Boat Shed has a fine reputation for its fresh seafood cuisine – their crabs and crayfish are plucked live from big saltwater tanks. The restaurant building was originally a boat-building shed, and looks out over Nelson's harbour.

Glover's Vineyard _____

Although he particularly enjoys red wine, Dave Glover and his wife Penny also produce some white wines. They got into the winemaking business in 1984 and produced their first vintage in 1989. A New Zealander, Dave spent 16 years in Australia during which time he studied viticulture and winemaking at Wagga Wagga, in New South Wales. (He also happens to have a PhD in algebra.)

CHEZ EELCO COFFEEHOUSE

296 Trafalgar Street, Nelson
phone *(03) 548 7595*

'Eelco's' is legendary among those who know and love the area. Nearly 40 years ago Eelco Boswijc opened his European-style coffeehouse at the foot of the cathedral. He provided newspapers and encouraged visitors to linger over a game of chess or backgammon – this man knew about café society long before the nineties! Many local artists have had their first exhibition displayed on the coffeehouse walls. Much of the now-nostalgic sixties décor has remained unchanged for more than three decades, and it's still a wonderfully atmospheric place to linger. The nineties touch is that now you can access your email here.

Their estate vineyard, comprising just three hectares (although they do buy in fruit), is in the rolling hills of the Upper Moutere, and has a reputation for producing wines that are not shy on tannins. Dave is quick to point out that he's not aiming to achieve Australian-style reds. He likes the tannins because he wants his wines to have longevity. Visitors who have a taste for Wagner will particularly enjoy their visit to Glover's Vineyard.

☞ **Gardners Valley Road, Upper Moutere**
Phone/fax: (03) 543 2698
Email: dave@glovers-vineyard.co.nz
Website: www.glovers-vineyard.co.nz
Hours: October to May seven days 10am-5pm, June to September by appointment.
Eating/other facilities: none.
Owners: Dave and Penny Glover
Winemaker: Dave Glover

Wines produced
○ Glover's Richmond Chardonnay, $20-22
Glover's Richmond Riesling, $16-18
Glover's Moutere Sauvignon Blanc, $16-18

● Glover's Moutere Cabernet Sauvignon, $30-32
Glover's Moutere Pinot Noir, $30-33
Glover's Spring Grove Shiraz, $30-32

Greenhough Vineyard _____

The wine Andrew Greenhough is really passionate about is pinot noir and he's concentrating his present efforts on growing the grape in his own vineyard. He also grows chardonnay and riesling, but buys in his sauvignon blanc from local growers. When he and Jenny Wheeler bought their Waimea Plains property in 1990 he spent the first five years replanting and increasing volumes and, as he puts it, 'learning the business. There was a bit of leeway in our early days – it was a good time to be learning on the job.' Along the way Andrew worked a vintage in Burgundy. Now, he says, the situation is much more competitive.

Whatever the situation, you get the sense that this winemaker will always strive to get better and better. Andrew is now looking to expand the business. Most Greenhough wines are exported or are available only through restaurants – reason enough to make the trip to the winery itself.

☞ **Pattons Road, RD1 Hope, Nelson**

Phone: (03) 542 3868

Fax: (03) 542 3462

Hours: open weekends from Labour weekend until Easter. Between 27 December and 24 February open seven days, 1pm-5pm.

Eating/other facilities: none.

Owners: Jenny Wheeler and Andrew Greenhough

Winemaker: Andrew Greenhough

Wines produced

○ Greenhough Nelson Chardonnay, $19-21
Greenhough Hope Chardonnay, $29-32
Greenhough Nelson Riesling, $16-18
Greenhough Nelson Sauvignon Blanc, $16-18

● Greenhough Pinot Noir, $24-26
Greenhough Hope Pinot Noir, $32-35

THE GRAPE ESCAPE CAFÉ AND WINE BAR

McShane Road, Richmond, Nelson
phone *(03) 544 4054*

Open in summer seven days 10.30am to 5pm, and in winter Wednesday to Sunday 11am to 4pm, for lunches, morning and afternoon teas, or for private evening functions by arrangement.

JESTER HOUSE CAFÉ

Coastal Highway 60, Tasman
phone *(03) 526 6742*

Forty minutes out of Nelson along the Coastal Highway, your eye will be caught by the sign of a smiling jester. Make your way over the little wooden footbridge and the first curiosity of Jester House greets you – the sight of tame eels swirling about in the creek. The food here is homemade and tasty, and the craft works on sale are interesting, although some are decidedly eccentric.

JACARANDA PARK

*College Street West,
Motueka*
phone (03) 528 7777

This garden café is situated in park gardens on a hilltop with the most stunning views of the Motueka River Valley and Tasman Bay. The fully licensed café is in an adobe building and also has a gallery room with a permanent exhibition of classic bronze sculptures, as well as contemporary pieces.

Holmes Brothers

David and Heather Holmes planted their vineyard in 1991 and from the start decided to manage it organically. This decision was partly because of their own philosophy to use fewer pesticides and synthetic fertilisers and part good business sense – they had seen a surge in demand for organic products in the late 80s and are seeing it again now. The vineyard was the first in the South Island to get Bio-Gro certification and it is unique in the region.

These certified organic wines are released under the Richmond Plains label – look for the distinctive design of the emerging frond of the New Zealand silver fern. The sauvignon blanc has had particular mention and the Escapade White took a bronze in the 1998 Air New Zealand Wine Awards. David Holmes has a distinct twinkle in the eye when he tells you that 'escapade' has the dictionary definition of 'a reckless adventure'. The Escapade Red has a wonderful complexity of flavours, including a tantalising hint of sandalwood.

Holmes Brothers and Te Mania Estate have combined tasting facilities, as well as joining forces in the Grape Escape Café, where you can get a delicious lunch. In the winery next door to the café David and Jon Harrey of Te Mania are enthusiastic about sharing their knowledge of winemaking, tasting, and even spitting. There is even a locally made ceramic official Grape Escape spittoon in which to practise the art! The café is housed in an historic cottage set in landscaped gardens next to one of the winery's vineyards. Small wonder that this place is so popular.

☞ **The Grape Escape Winery and Cellar,
McShane Rd, Richmond, Nelson**
Phone/fax: (03) 544 4054
Email: wine@hbd.co.nz
Website: www.nzwine.com/holmes/

Hours: for tasting and buying wines, same as café.

Eating/other facilities: The Grape Escape Café and Winebar is open in summer seven days 10.30am to 5pm and in winter Wednesday to Sunday 11am to 4pm. There is also an art gallery and crafts shop, a pottery, a plant nursery and gardens.

Owners: David and Heather Holmes

Winemaker: Jane Cooper

Wines produced

○ Richmond Plains Chardonnay, $19-21
Richmond Plains Escapade White, $15-17
Richmond Plains Sauvignon Blanc, $17-19

● Richmond Plains Escapade Red, $24-27
Richmond Plains Pinot Noir, $19-22

Moutere Hills Vineyard _____

The Nelson region worked its magic on English couple Simon and Alison Thomas in 1993. They'd had a year in Australia and a couple of years in Wellington but the plan had been to return to England. They changed their minds when a farm block came up for sale in Upper Moutere.

Both teachers, they had also been interested in wine for a long time. Simon, with a background in chemistry and geology, had been a hobby winemaker and they were enthusiastic about getting into the business. 'People come in with a smile and leave with a smile – it's a pretty nice line in retail.'

Because their 26.6 hectares was the home block of the farm, they inherited lots of old barns and sheds. The old shearing shed and sheep yards became the winery. 'It was a lot of hard work but it's given the place a lot of character. It's a bit rough around the edges but people seem to like that. It's certainly not a corporate look!'

They're determined to give visitors a relaxing and

MAPUA NATURE SMOKE CAFÉ
Shed 3, Mapua Wharf
phone (03) 540 2280

Along the Coastal Highway to Motueka is the village of Mapua, and at the far end of the village is the small Mapua Wharf. There you will discover a seaside café and smokehouse specialising in fishy dishes that include hot smoked salmon, mussels and a selection of mouth-watering fish pâtés. If you have time to stop this is an excellent place to partake of a crisp bottle of local wine and one of the delicious dishes on the menu, while the tide ebbs and flows past the window. If you are in a hurry you can buy pâté and other specialties to take away.

AWAROA LODGE AND CAFÉ

*Awaroa Inlet, PO Box 72,
Takaka, Golden Bay
phone/fax (03) 528 8758*

$-$$$

The beautiful bush walks and gorgeous beaches of Abel Tasman National Park are literally the homeland of the lodge. You can get to it by water taxi (embark at Kaiteriteri or Marahau and allow up to two-and-a-half hours for a one-way journey) or, if you're fit and have more time to spare than just a weekend, you can walk in through the park or even kayak up the coastline of this special part of New Zealand. It's certainly worth the effort! The lodge provides a range of accommodation from backpackers hostel to private rooms and individual chalets, and the café serves delicious locally grown produce.

enjoyable experience. They've established a playground for children and a lovely garden for visitors to sit in and have a light lunch or just take part in a wine tasting. 'We serve platters with high quality, simple food, a lot of it local. It's very much food to accompany the wine, not the other way around.'

Simon is aiming for quality in all his wines, but he's putting a lot of emphasis on producing an excellent pinot noir. He's just planted some pinot gris which he believes has a lot of potential, and he's producing a sauvignon blanc that is partially barrel fermented. 'It's a little different,' he says.

☞ **Sunrise Valley, RD1 Upper Moutere, Nelson**

Phone/fax: (03) 543 2288

Hours: for tasting and buying wines, 11am-6pm October to Easter.

Eating/other facilities: light lunches are available. Visitors are welcome to bring a picnic. There's a large garden and play area.

Owners: Simon and Alison Thomas

Winemaker: Simon Thomas

Wines produced

○ Moutere Hills Chardonnay, $18-21
Moutere Hills Riesling, $15-17
Moutere Hills Rosé, $16-18
Moutere Hills Sauvignon Blanc, $16-18

● Moutere Hills Merlot/Cabernet Franc, $17-20

Neudorf Vineyards _____

Established in 1978, this is one of the leading wineries in the country. Tim and Judy Finn were amongst the earliest to venture into winemaking in the Upper Moutere, and their Moutere Chardonnay and Moutere Riesling are regarded as classic wines.

Both Tim and Judy have rural connections. Tim graduated with a masters degree in science and was an advisory officer with the Ministry of Agriculture and Fisheries. Judy was a rural reporter for radio. They decided to get into the wine industry in its early days in New Zealand and their shared vision was to make world-class wines. And they export to the UK, Australia, the USA and France.

Tim says it's still a buzz and he's learning all the time. 'You just achieve new levels. I want to be small, I want to be excellent and I need to be excellent. New Zealanders have got a very good palate.' Judy says he's a perfectionist. The vineyard and winery are in a picturesque setting, and Neudorf was the first winery in New Zealand to serve food. In the very early days visitors were invited to bring their own picnic lunch; then they started to serve delicious light lunches themselves. However, they've now decided to return to the idea of people bringing a picnic. But Judy is keen to establish some regular tasting sessions which can be used by visitors as a real learning experience. If you fall in love with their wines, it's a good idea to get on their mailing list.

☞ **Neudorf Rd, Upper Moutere**

Phone: (03) 543 2643

Fax: (03) 543 2955

Email: neudorf@ts.co.nz

Hours: September to May, Monday to Saturday 10am-5pm.

Eating/other facilities: visitors are welcome to enjoy their own picnic at the vineyard tables.

Owners: Tim and Judy Finn

Winemaker: Tim Finn

Assistant winemaker: Mike Weersing

BRONTE LODGE

Bronte Road East, RD1, Mapua (off Coastal Highway 60)
phone (03) 540 2422
fax (03) 540 2637
email: margaret@ brontelodge.co.nz

$$$

With wonderful views over the Waimea inlet, this luxury smokefree B&B (though guests are welcome to smoke in the garden) is only a half-hour's drive out of Nelson on the route that takes you to the heart of the Waimea Plains vineyards and wineries. It has four extremely comfortable, stylish units available and the breakfast menu is mouth-watering. Also on offer are a tennis court, swimming pool, petanque court and the use of a canoe. Bruce and Margaret Fraser, who own the lodge, have planted half a hectare in vines and plan to serve their own house wines in due course.

CALIFORNIA HOUSE INN

*29 Collingwood Street,
Nelson*

phone/fax: (03) 548 4173

$$–$$$

This lovely old house, which has an Historic Places classification for its architectural significance, is fairly central. The house was built in 1893, and all the rooms have appropriate period furniture. California House is just a short walk from the centre of the city.

Wines produced

○ Neudorf Moutere Chardonnay, $37-40
Neudorf Nelson Chardonnay, $23-25
Neudorf Brightwater Riesling, $16-18
Neudorf Moutere Riesling, $18-20
Neudorf Sauvignon Blanc, $17-20

● Neudorf Moutere Pinot Noir, $32-36
Neudorf Moutere Reserve Pinot Noir, $38-42

Richmond Plains
(*See* Holmes Brothers)

Ruby Bay Wines

Driving up Korepo Road, you can look out over Ruby Bay and across the water to Nelson city. The same stunning view can be enjoyed from this estate vineyard, and if you drive down the hill a little way you will reach the winery. There is also a restaurant with seating both indoors and out at rustic tables on a gentle slope edged with an enchanting perennial garden.

The winery began life as the Karepo winery in the mid-1970s, but in 1989 new owners gave it a new name, Ruby Bay Wines. In 1999 it again changed hands and is now run by Phil Croy and Anita Ewart-Croy.

Anita's family had a vineyard in the Burnham area, a little south of Christchurch. This had been her incentive to take up winemaking and viticulture. Phil had worked on the marketing side of the wine industry, but decided he wanted to extend his knowledge, and went to Roseworthy College in Australia. The couple had already set the date for their wedding when the opportunity to take on Ruby Bay Wines arose. They took over the vineyard just two weeks later on the 13th of February. As Anita says, 'It was something of a whirlwind wedding!'

Their enthusiasm is infectious, and they certainly intend to make the most of their good fortune. Both Phil and Anita are keen to maintain the restaurant, serving simple but delicious food. Their first wines are a sauvignon blanc and a rosé.

☞ **Korepo Road, Upper Moutere**

Phone: (03) 540 2825

Fax: (03) 540 2105

Email: rubybay@xtra.co.nz

Hours: for tasting and buying wines, seven days a week all year round, 11am-6pm. Tours by arrangement. Wine club meets every month.

Eating/other facilities: outside garden dining and large covered dining area. Light lunch menu Monday-Friday, extensive brunch/lunch menu Saturday-Sunday 11am-3pm, seven days. Children's playground.

Owners: Bob and Lynne Croy, Philip Croy and Anita Ewart-Croy

Winemaker: Anita Ewart-Croy

Wines produced

○ Ruby Bay Chardonnay, $18-20
Ruby Bay Pinot Rosé, $15-17
Ruby Bay Sauvignon Blanc, $15-17
Ruby Bay Home Block Sauvignon Blanc, $16-18
Ruby Bay Tom's Block Sauvignon Blanc, $15-17

● Ruby Bay Merlot/Cabernet Franc, $18-20
Ruby Bay Pinot Noir, $15-17
Ruby Bay Reserve Pinot Noir, $22-25

DOONE COTTAGE

RD1 Motueka
phone/fax (03) 526 8740
email: doone-cottage@xtra.co.nz
website: http://nz.com/webnz/bbnz/doone.htm

$-$$

Half an hour inland from Motueka, on State Highway 61 (between Motueka and Tapawera), this is the ideal homestay for those wanting to spend some quiet time in one of the region's beautiful river valleys. Doone Cottage is a charming 100-year-old home that looks out across the Motueka Valley to the Mount Arthur range. For those who like fishing for trout there are six rivers in the locality! Stan and Glen Davenport are truly welcoming hosts.

SANS SOUCI

Contact Vera and Rito Balzer
Richmond Road, RD1,
Pohara, Takaka
phone (03) 525 8663

$

As its name implies, this is a place to relax and forget the stresses of the office. Although there are no wineries to visit in Golden Bay there are plenty of panoramic beaches and secluded rivers. Travel from Motueka over the Takaka Hills and make your way to Pohara Beach, on the road to the Abel Tasman National Park. This is about two-and-a-half hours from Nelson city so you will want to stay the night, and what better place than Sans Souci. The units are built of clay brick and each has French doors out to an individual patio. There is also a licensed restaurant.

Seifried Estate

Hermann and Agnes Seifried are acknowledged as the pioneers of the Nelson winemaking industry. Hermann planted his first vineyard in the Upper Moutere district in 1974. Now Seifried Estate has 50 hectares of vineyards, some in the clay soils of the Moutere and others drawing their character from the stony soils of the Waimea Plains. The estate produces over half the wine that comes from the Nelson region.

The Austrian eagle on the Seifried Estate label proudly declares where Hermann hails from. He came to New Zealand in 1971, having worked as a winemaker in South Africa. Those who visited this area in the early days of Seifried's wines would make a point of travelling to the Upper Moutere to taste his delicious rieslings or the scrumptious Gewürztraminer Ice Wine. In those days tasting and buying was done in a simple area set aside next to the winery. Today Seifried Estate's wines can be enjoyed in the beautifully designed tasting room.

In the mid-1990s Hermann and Agnes built an extensive vineyard restaurant on the plains area near Richmond. Here you can sit inside or at umbrella-shaded tables outside the restaurant for lunch or dinner. You can relax in the cocktail bar or throw a private party in 'Vines', a function room with a stunning view of the vineyards and surrounding countryside.

Seifried Estate's wines have been spectacularly successful, both in New Zealand and in export sales around the world, and their chardonnay won gold at the 1998 International Wine Competition in London.

☛ **Redwood Road (Coastal Highway at Rabbit Island turnoff), Appleby**

Phone: (03) 544 5599

Fax: (03) 544 5522

Email: seifried@winesnelson.co.nz

Hours: winery open 10am–5pm daily all year round.

Eating/other facilities: Vineyard Restaurant and Café, open same hours as winery. For bookings phone (03) 544 1555 or fax (03) 544 1700.

Owners: Agnes and Hermann Seifried

Winemaker: Daniel Schwerzenbach

Wines produced

○ Old Coach Road Chardonnay, $13-15
Old Coach Road Unoaked Chardonnay, $12-13
Old Coach Road Classic Dry White, $8-9
Seifried Chardonnay, $16-18
Winemakers Collection Barrique Fermented
Chardonnay '97, $25-28
Seifried Gewürztraminer, $13-15
Winemakers Collection Gewürztraminer Ice Wine
375ml, $20-22
Seifried Riesling, $12-13
Winemakers Collection Riesling, $16-18
Winemakers Collection Riesling Ice Wine 375ml,
$16-18
Old Coach Road Sauvignon Blanc, $12-13
Seifried Sauvignon Blanc, $15-17
Seifried Sparkling Sekt, $8-9
Old Coach Road White Autumn, $9-11

● Seifried Cabernet Merlot, $16-18
Seifried Cabernet Sauvignon, $16-18
Old Coach Road Classic Pinot/Cabernet, $9-11
Seifried Pinot Noir, $16-18

SOUTH STREET COTTAGES

phone/fax (03) 540 2769
email: south.street.cottages
@xtra.co.nz
website: www.friars.co.nz/
hosts/sthstcottages.html

$$$

Peter and Jeanette Hancock are part owners of Pomona Ridge Vineyard, on the hills above Ruby Bay, which in 1999 they leased out to another winery to give themselves more time to concentrate on their hospitality business in the city. They now have three historic cottages available for accommodation, and have restored them all beautifully, retaining their old world charm plus all the comforts anyone could want. Biddle Cottage, Briar Cottage and Dillon Cottage each has a slightly different character. They are absolutely centrally placed, very close to Nelson Cathedral.

Te Mania Estate _____

Te Mania (Maori for 'the plains') is situated on the Waimea Plains close to Richmond on the local stony, free-draining soils that have proved to be ideal for the production of grapes. It used to be said that you didn't grow grapes on

Department of Conservation, Cnr King Edward and High Streets, Motueka
phone (03) 528 9117

New Zealand's smallest national park, Abel Tasman, is largely covered in beech forest plus some rain forest and nikau palms. It's breathtaking, but if you 'want to be alone' avoid the main holiday period. There are tracks to accommodate many levels of fitness, and you can choose between a day trip into the park or the complete three- to four-day trip between Marahau and Awaroa. Along the way there are beautiful golden sand beaches, most of which are safe for swimming.

SEA KAYAKING

Kayaking along the coast of the Abel Tasman Park is a great way to explore its many coves and beaches. It's also a chance to see at close hand penguins, dolphins, seals and native birds. Most companies provide tuition and easy trips for beginners. Contact local information centres for details.

the plains, you grew apples. Jon Harrey smiles at how the received wisdom of the past has been proved so wrong.

Jon had a background in property valuation and came to one of those life-changing crossroads in 1990. The upshot was that Jon and his wife Cheryl bought 4.6 hectares of land to start up their small family vineyard.

Jon says his interest is in growing the quality grapes that give quality wines. He likes to be the 'assistant winemaker', but he admits that over the years 'a passion has taken over' when it comes to managing the vineyard. They haven't adopted organic practices, but aim to have as minimal an impact on the environment as is sustainable. Not surprisingly, therefore, they have teamed up with Richmond Plains in The Grape Escape Winery and Cellar where you can have a great time tasting and learning – as well as popping next door into the Grape Escape Café for a tasty lunch.

Their first production of pinot noir was released in 1999, and Jon says to look for 'sweet cherry and aromatic fruitcake aromas with hints of savoury oak'.

☛ **McShanes Road, RD1 Richmond, Nelson**
Phone/fax: (03) 544 4541
Email: temania@ts.co.nz
Website: www.nzwine.com/temania
Hours: for tasting and buying wines, summer 10am-5pm, winter 11am-4pm.
Eating/other facilities: The Grape Escape Café is open daily for lunches, morning and afternoon teas, or for private evening functions by arrangement. Adjoining is an art and craft shop, a garden nursery, and a playground.
Owners: Jon and Cheryl Harrey
Winemaker: Jane Cooper

Wines produced

○ Te Mania Chardonnay, $18-20
Te Mania Riesling, $15-17
Te Mania Riesling Ice Wine, $20-22
Te Mania Sauvignon Blanc, $16-18

● Te Mania Merlot, $20-22
Te Mania Montage, $16-18
Te Mania Pinot Noir, $20-23

Wai-iti River Vineyard ————

Philip Woollaston grew up in this region but spent quite a few years away from it. In the early 1990s he and his wife Chan were in Nairobi, where Philip was working as an environmental advisor for the United Nations. They returned to New Zealand, and in 1993 established a small vineyard on the Waimea Plains in a pocket of the free-draining gravel soil of an old riverbed. And 'small' is fine with them – their aim is to produce modest quantities of high quality wines.

Their first vintage was in 1996, using estate-grown grapes for all their wines except the riesling. They are planting riesling, but the first of this wine they produced, in 1998, was made from locally sourced fruit. It had very prominent citrus flavours, and Philip says the 1999 is even better. He is also particularly enthusiastic about their 1997 pinot noir, which is very flavoursome and has a 'superb tannic structure'.

In the past Philip and Chan have concentrated their energies purely on the growing of the grapes and the making of the wine, but now they're developing a tasting room. The vineyard is in a very attractive location with fantastic views of the hills, and visitors can picnic on the property.

SCENIC FLIGHTS

Abel Tasman Aviation Nelson Ltd, Motueka Airfield, College Street, Motueka freephone 0800 304 560 phone/fax (03) 528 6767

The ultimate for an overview of this lovely region. Ideal for giving a sense of perspective to those great bush walks.

GARDEN TOURS

Because of the excellent climate there are a lot of enviable gardens here. Many of them are open to visitors in the summer months. Information centres carry a brochure giving details.

CERAMICS AND POTTERY

Some of New Zealand's most widely acclaimed ceramic artists live here, and many open their studios to the public. There is a 'pottery trail', where you can see anything from beautiful domestic ware to stunning sculptures. The information centres carry brochures and the local guidebook *Art in Its Own Place* is also available.

WHITEWATER RAFTING

Another way to see the wonderful scenery and to get a real buzz at the same time is to put on a wetsuit and helmet and raft down the local rivers. There are a number of good rafting companies covering the Nelson and West Coast rivers. Information centres carry details.

HÖGLUND ART GLASS

Korurangi Farm, Lansdowne Road, Richmond
phone (03) 544 6500
fax (03) 544 9935
email: hoglund@ts.co.nz

There is a certain magic to glass, and to be able to watch it being blown, as you can here, is entrancing. Ola and Marie Höglund have an inspired design sense and their work is acquiring an international reputation. But a visit to their Korurangi Farm has other advantages too. They have established a café and wine bar, and serve local gourmet delights. And you can sit outside in their lovely garden, which is also home to several peacocks.

☞ **Livingston Road, Waimea West (near Brightwater)**

Phone/fax: (03) 542 3205

Email: wai-iti.river@clear.net.nz

Hours: 10am-6pm daily (summer season) or by appointment.

Eating/other facilities: outdoor tasting/picnic area.

Owners: Chan and Philip Woollaston

Winemaker: Dave Glover

Wines produced

○ Wai-iti River Chardonnay, $18-20
Wai-iti River Riesling, $17-19
Wai-iti River Big Creek White, $12-13

● Wai-iti River Cabernet Sauvignon, $21-24
Wai-iti River Pinot Noir, $18-20
Wai-iti River Reserve Pinot Noir, $30-33

Waimea Estates _____

Waimea Estates, established in 1997, is a family owned and operated business. Trevor and Robyn Bolitho are passionate in their conviction that the Waimea Plains – and the Nelson area generally – has terrific potential for winemaking. They have four vineyards totalling 76 hectares, making the estate one of the largest in New Zealand. While they sell a lot of their grapes, all the wine produced on the estate is from their own vineyards.

From the start Waimea Estate has had all its wines ranked in the top three of their respective varieties at the annual Air New Zealand Wine Awards. So there are fine wines to try and an excellent selection of Nelson's finest produce in the café. But if you want your alfresco lunching to be 'sur l'herbe', ring beforehand and you can order a picnic basket complete with food, wine and a blanket.

☛ **148 Main Road, Hope**

Phone/fax: (03) 544 6385

Email: jo@waimeaestates.co.nz

Hours: 10am-10pm, seven days.

Eating/other facilities: café with indoor/outdoor seating, 10am-10pm, seven days, picnic baskets available. Petanque area.

Owners: Trevor and Robyn Bolitho

Winemakers: Sam Weaver and Jane Cooper

Wines produced

○ Waimea Estate Chardonnay, $17-19
Waimea Estate Riesling, $14-16
Waimea Estate Sauvignon Blanc, $16-18

● Waimea Estate Cabernet Merlot, $17-20

Mostly Closed to the Public

Spencer Hill Estate _____

☛ **phone** (03) 543 2031

email: spencer.hill@clear.net.nz

Described by some as unconventional, these single vineyard wines made by ex-pat American Phil Jones have won an impressive number of awards and have an enthusiastic following.

THE BISHOP SUTER ART GALLERY

208 Bridge Street, Nelson
phone (03) 548 4699
fax (03) 548 1236
email: suter@netaccess.co.nz

The third art museum established in New Zealand, the 'Suter' houses an excellent collection of works by some of New Zealand's most respected artists. It is also a showcase for a wide variety of local art and ceramics – the ideal starting point before exploring the art trails of the region. The gallery has a glassed-in café, which extends into the adjacent Queen's Gardens, as well as theatres showing plays and movies.

SOUTH PACIFIC DISTILLERY

258 Wakefield Quay, Nelson
phone (03) 546 6822
fax (03) 546 6826

Sipping of a different kind! Fine producers of rum, South Pacific offers free tastings and all their products are distilled from 100 percent grain or cane products. No artificial flavourings or preservatives are used.

FAREWELL SPIT

*Farewell Spit Nature Tours,
Collingwood, Golden Bay
freephone 0800 250 500
fax (03) 524 8091*

This 25-kilometre 'finger' is the longest sandspit in the country. Centuries of exposure to the forces of wind and sea have created a magnificent landscape. The area is also an internationally renowned bird sanctuary.

WATER TAXIS

Water taxis make regular runs into the beautiful bays of the Abel Tasman National Park. You can embark either at Kaiteriteri or Marahau and you need to allow up to two-and-a-half hours for a one-way journey. The following operators offer regular services.

*Abel Tasman National Park
Enterprises
265 High Street, Motueka,
phone (03) 528 7801
fax (03) 528 6087
freephone 0800 223 582*

*Abel Tasman Seafaris Aquataxi
Marahau
phone (03) 527 8083
fax (03) 527 8282
freephone 0800 278 282*

The Grape Escape Winery and Cellar, Nelson

Bush walking, Nelson

Moutere Hills Vineyard, Nelson

Sea kayaking, Marlborough Sounds, Nelson

The Denton Winery, Nelson

ABEL TASMAN ENTERPRISES

Homestay, Nelson

Cloudy Bay Winery, Marlborough

KEVIN JUDD PHOTOGRAPHY

marlborough

This is the country's largest wine-growing region and the one that first put New Zealand on the world's 'wine map'. The town of Blenheim, hub of the Marlborough region, is one of the sunniest spots in the country, frequently recording more sunshine hours per year than anywhere else. A variety of soil types, plentiful sunshine, long autumns and crisp, cool winters in the region, plus the creativity and talent of the winemakers, have proved a recipe for wines of international standing.

The winemaking industry in Marlborough began as recently as the 1970s, but is developing at an extraordinary rate and has a reputation for producing some mouth-watering wines. Marlborough's succulent sauvignon blanc has put this region on the world wine map. One British wine writer described it as 'unbelievably memorable'!

Some of New Zealand's most prestigious wine-producing companies have now established themselves in the area. Cloudy Bay and Hunter's wines are probably the most well known outside New Zealand – and what a buzz it is to be able to visit these wineries. But some very exciting boutique wineries have also emerged in the region. Often these have developed because grapegrowers contracted to the big companies have been bitten by the bug and made their own way into winemaking

A visit to Marlborough is a chance to sample a wonderful range of truly delicious wines. The soils of the area range from fertile deep silt loams to shallow, stony ground. The resulting differences in grape flavours are what give Marlborough wines such exciting variety.

Marlborough is also a very beautiful region. It is bordered by the Inland Kaikoura Ranges – mountains set against the sky, dramatic in bright sunshine or soft cloud, when they take on mysterious shades of deep blue. The

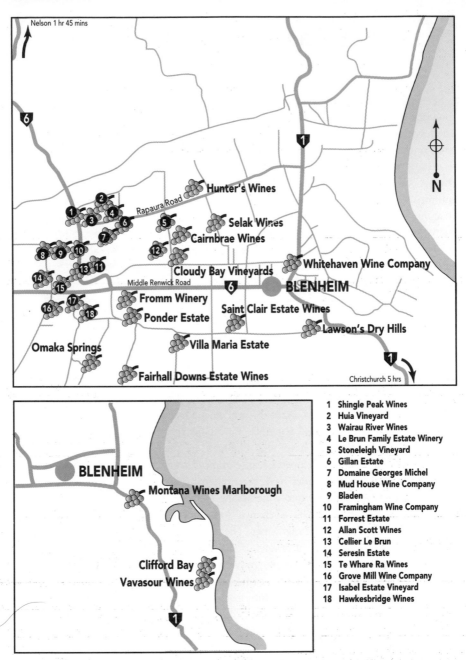

Nelson 1 hr 45 mins

N

6

1

Hunter's Wines

Rapaura Road

2

1

4

3

6

Selak Wines

5

7

Cairnbrae Wines

8 9 10

12

Whitehaven Wine Company

13 11

Cloudy Bay Vineyards

14

Middle Renwick Road

15

6

BLENHEIM

17

Fromm Winery

16

Saint Clair Estate Wines

18

Ponder Estate

Lawson's Dry Hills

Omaka Springs

Villa Maria Estate

1

Christchurch 5 hrs

Fairhall Downs Estate Wines

BLENHEIM

Montana Wines Marlborough

Clifford Bay
Vavasour Wines

1

1 Shingle Peak Wines
2 Huia Vineyard
3 Wairau River Wines
4 Le Brun Family Estate Winery
5 Stoneleigh Vineyard
6 Gillan Estate
7 Domaine Georges Michel
8 Mud House Wine Company
9 Bladen
10 Framingham Wine Company
11 Forrest Estate
12 Allan Scott Wines
13 Cellier Le Brun
14 Seresin Estate
15 Te Whare Ra Wines
16 Grove Mill Wine Company
17 Isabel Estate Vineyard
18 Hawkesbridge Wines

ranges drop down to the Wairau Plains, where these days you're likely to see almost mesmeric rows of vines. And, of course, there are also the deep waters of the magical Marlborough Sounds. Wonderful for sailing and fishing, or simply to put in at enchanting coves to laze on golden beaches. If you prefer fresh water, the area also has some picturesque picnic spots and swimming holes on the lakes and rivers. Small wonder that there are quite a number of winemakers who came to visit and simply stayed!

 Blenheim
2 High Street
PO Box 880
phone (03) 578 9904
fax (03) 578 6084
email: blm-info@clear.net.nz

Picton
Foreshore
PO Box 165
phone (03) 573 7477
fax (03) 573 5021

AUTHOR'S FAVOURITES

Allan Scott Sauvignon Blanc

Cloudy Bay Chardonnay

Framingham Riesling

Grove Mill Gewürztraminer

Hunter's Sauvignon Blanc

Lawson's Dry Hills Riesling

Ponder Estate Riesling

REGIONAL HIGHLIGHTS

HUNTER'S GARDEN MARLBOROUGH

Held in the second weekend in November, this is one of New Zealand's premier events for garden lovers. It includes workshops, tours and social activities.

Contact Denise Shaw
phone (03) 577 5500
fax (03) 577 5501

PICTON SOUNDS SPRING SCHOOL

A three-day September offering of literary and artistic workshops and courses.

Contact Rosalie Matthews
phone (03) 573 8553

the
wineries

Marlborough has an excellent reputation for its produce, whether it's 'fruit of the sea' or goodies from the land. Many of the best places to eat in Marlborough are the wineries, but its gourmet reputation is also reflected in a number of other excellent cafés and restaurants, where you can enjoy fine dining or more casual bistro-style meals, depending on your mood.

Allan Scott Wines and Estates

Allan Scott has come a long way from his first job in the wine industry as a vineyard labourer. That was in 1973 when Montana Wines established themselves in Marlborough. He'd only been doing that for a month when he became vineyard foreman – clearly this man had struck out in the right career direction. As a viticulturist with Montana and then Corbans, New Zealand's two largest wine-producing companies, he acquired the wide experience and skills that have helped to make his own business such a success. In 1990 he launched his own label with his release of the wine that Marlborough is famed for – sauvignon blanc. Allan's wines have an excellent name, and a trip to the winery is well worth the visit. And not only for the wines. The handsome winery is constructed from local timbers and rammed earth as is the restaurant, which has a reputation as good as that of the wine.

☞ **Jackson's Road, Blenheim**
 Phone: (03) 572 9054
 Fax: (03) 572 9053

Email: scott.wine@xtra.co.nz

Website: www.allanscott.com

Hours: daily 9am-5pm.

Eating/other facilities: Twelve Trees Vineyard Restaurant open 9am-5pm daily.

Owners: Allan and Catherine Scott

Winemaker: Greg Trought

Wines produced

○ Allan Scott Marlborough Chardonnay, $19-21
  Allan Scott Prestige Marlborough Chardonnay, $25-28
  Allan Scott Méthode Traditionelle Blanc de Blancs, $24-27
  Allan Scott Marlborough Riesling, $14-16
  Allan Scott Autumn Riesling 375ml, $30-33
  Allan Scott Marlborough Sauvignon Blanc, $16-19

● Allan Scott Marlborough Merlot, $22-24
  Twelve Trees Merlot, $18-20
  Allan Scott Marlborough Pinot Noir, $22-25

Bladen

Established in 1997, this is a relative newcomer as a winery in the region, though Dave Macdonald and Chris Lowes have been grapegrowers since 1989. They had been travelling in Europe in the mid-1980s and decided that the wine industry was the thing for them. Bladen specialises in white wine.

☛ **Conders Bend Road, Renwick**

Phone: (03) 572 9417

Fax: (03) 572 9217

Email: bladen@voyager.co.nz

Hours: October to end of February, daily noon-5pm.

BELLAFICO CAFFE WINE BAR

17 Maxwell Road, Blenheim
phone (03) 577 6072

This award-winning restaurant is in the centre of Blenheim. The cuisine is Mediterranean/pan-Pacific. Fully licensed and BYO. Open Monday to Saturday all year 9am to late, except during December when they are open seven days.

BLENHEIM COUNTRY LODGE HOTEL

Cnr of Alfred and Henry Streets, Blenheim
phone (03) 578 5079

'Seymours' is an award-winning restaurant in this family owned hotel. It has twice been winner of the 'Marlborough Chamber of Commerce Licensed Restaurant' award and the delicious food in pleasant surroundings make it worth a visit.

CORK & KEG

Inkerman Street, Renwick
phone (03) 572 9328

It's hard to believe that this pub is only five years old. It was designed to look like a 100-year-old English pub, and it does! Manager Bill Penfold (who arrived from London many years ago) says the Cork & Keg is the 'most English pub in New Zealand'. It's part of the Renwick Brewery that produces beer and cider and has an association with Cellier Le Brun. They have a blackboard menu – 'a pub grub board' – and serve things like little English pork pies and ploughman's lunches. They also have a beer garden and visitors are welcome to bring their own food, including things to cook on the pub barbecue. Open 7 days from 11am to midnight.

Eating/other facilities: none.

Owners: Dave Macdonald and Chris Lowes

Winemaker: Simon Waghorn

Wines produced

○ Bladen Gewürztraminer, $19-22
  Bladen Pinot Gris, $18-20
  Bladen Riesling, $15-17
  Bladen Sauvignon Blanc, $15-17

Cairnbrae Wines ───────────

Daphne and Murray Brown of Cairnbrae were early off the mark in seeing Marlborough's wine-producing potential. They established their vineyard in 1980 and for the first 11 years sold their fruit to local wineries. In the early 1990s they released the first wines under their own label, and have gone on to enjoy some well-rated successes. It's a great place to stop and have a meal. From the upstairs balcony, the views of the vines stretching across the valley add to the charm of the experience. The winery name is Gaelic for 'a stony pile on a hillside'. What more could you want for growing grapes!

☛ **Jacksons Road, Blenheim**

Phone: (03) 572 8018 (winery)

Fax: (03) 572 7018

Email: cairnbrae.wine@xtra.co.nz

Hours: for tasting and purchasing, daily 9am-5pm; reduced winter hours.

Eating/other facilities: café open daily 9am-5pm, phone (03) 572 8048.

Owners: Daphne and Murray Brown

Winemakers: Kim Crawford and Matt Thomson

Wines produced

○ Cairnbrae Chardonnay, $23-25
Cairnbrae Pinot Gris, $20-22
Cairnbrae Riesling, $17-20
Cairnbrae Late Harvest Riesling 375ml, $25-28
Cairnbrae Sauvignon Blanc, $17-19

Cellier Le Brun

A few bubbles with your brunch? Sit in Cellier Le Brun's Courtyard Café and enjoy the good life. Wander into the garden, or try your hand at that very French game, petanque.

Although he is now no longer involved with this vineyard, Daniel Le Brun, possibly the best known méthode traditionelle maker in New Zealand, was the one who drew the country's attention to Cellier Le Brun in a big way.

The vineyard was established in 1983. Cellars have been tunnelled into the hillside, where the wines can mature in a cool, temperature-controlled environment. Cellier Le Brun has gone on to produce a terrific range of méthode traditionelle wines. Cellier Le Brun's classic wines include Le Brun Vintage Brut, Le Brun Blanc de Blancs, and Le Brun NV Brut. The winery also produces, under the Terrace Road label, a line of modestly priced wines.

☛ **Terrace Road, Renwick**

Phone: (03) 572 8859

Fax: (03) 572 8814

Email: lebrun@xtra.co.nz

Hours: for tasting and purchasing, summer, 9am-5pm seven days; May-October Monday-Thursday 9am-4.30pm. Guided tours of the cellars also arranged.

DUKE'S RESTAURANT & BAR

20 Nelson Street, Blenheim
phone (03) 577 7333

Duke's is the restaurant at The Marlborough Hotel and it certainly makes the most of the grand old hotel's ambience. The chef at Duke's makes a point of serving the freshest of local produce, particularly game and seafood. Open seven days 7am to 10am and 6pm to 10pm.

D'URVILLE WINE BAR AND BRASSERIE

52 Queen Street, Blenheim
phone (03) 577 9944

Right in the heart of town, this delightful brasserie also serves Marlborough produce and offers dishes ranging from quail to salmon to corn-fed chicken. Fully licensed. Open 6am to midnight seven days.

EXPRESSO HOUSE

58 Auckland Street, Picton
phone (03) 573 7112

This delightful little cottage café is just a short stroll from the Interisland Ferry Terminal in Picton. It has seating outside in the courtyard as well as indoors. The interior is simple with polished floors and wood tables. Expresso House has an all-day blackboard menu and serves truly delicious gourmet meals made from fresh local produce. It has a BYO licence and in summer it is open from 11am for lunch and nightly for dinner. For the rest of the year Expresso is open every day except Wednesday.

Eating/other facilities: Courtyard Café for breakfast and lunch. Bubbly breakfast a speciality.

Owner: Tony Nightingale

Winemaker: Allan McWilliams

Wines produced

○ Daniel Le Brun Brut NV, $26-29
  Daniel Le Brun Brut NV 375ml, $15-17
  Daniel Le Brun Brut NV Magnum, $56-62
  Daniel Le Brun Brut NV Taché, $26-30
  Daniel Le Brun Vintage, $35-40
  Daniel Le Brun Blanc de Blancs, $35-40
  Daniel Le Brun Estate Millennium Cuvée, $39-45
  Terrace Road Classic Brut (méthode traditionelle)
    $18-21
  Terrace Road Chardonnay, $16-18
  Terrace Road Sauvignon Blanc, $15-17

● Terrace Road Pinot Noir, $16-19

Clifford Bay Estate _____

The first Clifford Bay Sauvignon Blanc, produced in 1997, won medals, great ratings and glowing comments. It was a remarkable success for a first vintage. And yet, in a story we hear quite often in the South Island, winemaking was a career about-turn for Eric Bowers and his wife Beverley who were previously involved in the petroleum business.

The couple established their vineyard in the lower Awatere Valley, where the land is silty, stony and free-draining – ideal for grapes. The vineyard sits on the terraces above the Awatere River with views that take in the mountains of the Inland Kaikoura Ranges to the southwest and the Pacific Ocean to the east. As well as sauvignon blanc, they have gone on to produce chardonnay and riesling. Clifford Bay has recently built premises for tasting and buying, and a café.

☛ **Rapaura Road, Blenheim**

Phone: (03) 578 4617

Fax: (03) 578 4619

Email: clifford.bay.estate@xtra.co.nz

Hours: for tasting and purchasing, 11am-4pm.

Eating/other facilities: café open 10am-4pm seven days.

Owners: Eric and Beverley Bowers, Graham and Thelma Cains, Chris Wilson

Winemaker: Glen Thomas

Wines produced
○ Clifford Bay Chardonnay, $17-20
Clifford Bay Riesling, $14-16
Clifford Bay Sauvignon Blanc, $16-18

Cloudy Bay Vineyards _____

Although New Zealand wines have a growing reputation around the world, there's still a way to go before the names of many of our wines come easily to the mind of anyone outside this country. The wines of Cloudy Bay are probably the only exception. International connections and smart marketing have certainly helped, but the high quality of these wines confirms that their reputation is well deserved. From the first release of its sauvignon blanc in 1985, Cloudy Bay has consistently produced excellent wines that have caused a lot of excitement.

The winery is named after the nearby bay, which turns cloudy when the Wairau River brings silt into it. Cloudy Bay's elegant label reflects the distant mountains of the area. The stony, well-drained soils of Marlborough have provided the magic flavours, but the magician is winemaker Kevin Judd. An Australian and a graduate of Roseworthy College, Kevin joined Cloudy Bay in 1985.

The venture had been the inspiration of another

THE KEKERENGU STORE

State Highway 1
phone (03) 575 8600

About half way between Blenheim and Kaikoura, when you reach the coastal stretch of the journey, is the tiny settlement of Kekerengu. Its main feature is a most attractive café called The Store, where you can turn your back on the busy highway and look along the rugged coastline or out over the Pacific Ocean. There is a wide verandah with seating or you can sit inside on colder winter days and be warmed by a large open fireplace. It's a great place to have a good coffee, a snack or a light meal. The Store is fully licensed, and open seven days 7.30am to late.

MARLBOROUGH TERRANEAN
31 High Street, Picton
phone (03) 573 7122

Terranean specialises in fresh seafood – always plentiful this close to the waters of the Marlborough Sounds. This is an ideal place for a meal when you've just disembarked from the Cook Strait ferry. Open seven days from 6pm.

THE MUSSEL BOYS RESTAURANT

73 Main Road, Havelock
phone (03) 574 2824

This is definitely a place for shellfish lovers. You can get fresh fish and wonderful chowders, but these 'boys' are mussel specialists. They have a fine reputation for their 'steamers' or 'grilled flats' and the greenshell mussels are harvested right there in the Marlborough Sounds each day. Fully licensed. Open seven days 11am-9pm in summer, 11am-7pm in winter.

Australian, David Hohnen. David was a part-owner of Cape Mentelle, a prestigious winery in Western Australia. His instinct told him that New Zealand sauvignon blanc was a wine waiting to be discovered. In 1990 when the French champagne house Veuve Clicquot-Ponsardin bought a majority share in Cape Mentelle, it also bought into the Cloudy Bay phenomenon. Both Cloudy Bay's chardonnay and its sauvignon blanc are regarded as classic wines, as is the méthode traditionelle, Pelorus Vintage. And for a very special treat, try a glass of the Late Harvest Riesling.

☛ **Jacksons Road, Blenheim**
Phone: (03) 572 8914
Fax: (03) 572 8065
Email: cloudybay@xtra.co.nz
Hours: 10am-4.30pm daily.
Eating/other facilities: none.
Owners: Cape Mentelle and David Hohnen
Winemaker: Kevin Judd

Wines produced
○ Cloudy Bay Chardonnay, $29-32
   Cloudy Bay Late Harvest Riesling 375ml, $22-25
   Cloudy Bay Sauvignon Blanc, $22-26
   Cloudy Bay Te Koko Sauvignon Blanc, $31-35
   Cloudy Bay Pelorus N.V., $32-35
   Cloudy Bay Pelorus Vintage, $38-43

● Cloudy Bay Pinot Noir, $29-33

Domaine Georges Michel _____
This is another of Marlborough's French connections. Georges Michel owns a winery in Beaujolais, and in the late 1990s bought the winery and vineyard of what was

once Merlen wines. This winery was very much part of Marlborough's winemaking history. It was begun by Almuth Lorenz, who had grown up in the Rheinhessen and as a child had worked in her parents' eight-hectare vineyard and winery. She studied at the Geisenheim Institute and came to New Zealand in the early 1980s. She had already established a reputation when she was Hunter's winemaker, but in 1987 she set out on her own, becoming well-known as a white wine specialist with a considerable following.

With the take-over by Georges Michel there are ongoing plans to update the winery. In the meantime, it's a lovely area and it's possible to enjoy a delicious café meal there.

☞ **Vintage Lane, Blenheim**

Phone: (03) 572 7230

Fax: (03) 572 7231

Email: georgesmichel@xtra.co.nz

Hours: for tasting and purchasing, summer 9am-5pm, winter 10am-4pm.

Eating/other facilities: The Gates vineyard café. Lunches served every day in summer, evening dining also available Friday and Saturday.

Owners: Georges Michel, Groupe Georges Michel

Winemaker: Guy Brac de la Perriere

Assistant winemaker: John McGirby

Wines produced
○ Domaine Georges Michel Chardonnay, $19-22
Domaine Georges Michel Sauvignon Blanc, $16-19

PADDY BARRY'S IRISH PUB

51 Scott Street, Blenheim
phone (03) 578 7470

Paddy Barry's has become famous for its platters. Try a 'Barry's Big' or 'Irish Sea' or find out what 'Murphs & Irish Strawberries' is. The pub has a relaxed atmosphere and you can eat either indoors or sitting on the balcony watching the world go by. Open seven days 11am until late.

PAYSANNE CAFÉ & BAR

The Forum Marketplace, Blenheim
Phone (03) 577 6278

The Forum Marketplace is right in the heart of Blenheim and upstairs, on a corner site of the building, is this café. It opens out onto two balconies that also have seating. Paysanne has a wood-burning oven so the specialty to go for is their gourmet pizza. The choices include 'Tandoori Chicken' and 'Venison and Cranberry'. In winter the café is closed on Sundays but open the rest of the week from 9am until late. From December to March it opens on Sunday as well, from 5pm to 10pm.

Fairhall Downs Estate Wines ____

Growing grapes for other wineries serves as a great apprenticeship. Fairhall Downs' family grapegrowing business was established in 1982. Ten years down the track they decided to make their own wines. They chose to concentrate on producing premium varietal wines, and Fairhall Downs has gone on to have tremendous success with these at wine competitions. Every vintage of sauvignon blanc has won awards, including a gold medal and trophy in 1998. The first chardonnay, released in 1997, took three silver medals in the following year.

☛ **814 Wrekin Road, Brancott Valley, Blenheim**
Phone: (03) 572 8356
Fax: (03) 572 8357
Email: fairhalldowns.wines@xtra.co.nz
Hours: by appointment only.
Eating/other facilities: none.
Owners: Ken and Jill Small, Stuart and Julie Smith
Winemaker: John Forrest

Wines produced
○ Fairhall Downs Chardonnay, $16-18
Fairhall Downs Pinot Gris, $20-23
Fairhall Downs Estate Sauvignon Blanc, $14-16

Forrest Estate Winery _____

In their first vintage in 1990, John and Brigid Forrest produced a cabernet rosé that won the champion rosé trophy for that year. It also brought Forrest Estate to the attention of the industry. The winery has gone on to establish itself as a producer of crisp whites and rich-flavoured reds. The couple have had other successful careers, John as a biochemist and Brigid in clinical medicine, but their interest in wine turned them in a new direction. Of course they bring their scientific skills to the venture but, for them, the creative side to winemaking is just as alluring. The winery itself has a stunning view across the plains to the Richmond Ranges. Call in on a Saturday and John is happy to talk about his winemaking philosophy of adding fullness and complexity to the distinctive, fresh, varietal flavours of Marlborough. During the summer, take time to enjoy a ploughman's lunch with your wine.

☞ **Blicks Road, Renwick**

Phone: (03) 572 9084

Fax: (03) 572 9086

Email: forrestj@voyager.co.nz

Hours: 10.30-4.30 daily. Closed weekends June-October. Meet the winemaker on Saturdays.

Eating/other facilities: ploughman's lunch served during summer.

Owners: John and Brigid Forrest

Winemaker: John Forrest

Wines produced

○ Forrest Estate Chardonnay, $19-22
Forrest Estate Riesling, $14-16
Forrest Estate Botrytised Riesling 375ml, $22-25
Forrest Estate Late Harvest Riesling 375ml, $15-18
Forrest Estate Rosé, $14-16
Forrest Estate Sauvignon Blanc, $15-17
Forrest Estate Sémillon, $14-16

● Forrest Estate Pinot Noir, $20-24

Many wineries also offer accommodation – see individual entries for details.

BROOMFIELD
35 Inkerman Street, Renwick
phone (03) 572 8162

$$$

Just 12 minutes out of Blenheim, this is another private getaway. Newly built of limewashed rammed earth, Broomfield is the two-storey home of Kaye and Gary Green. They have just one guestroom, upstairs looking out over the gardens, which include an interesting kitchen garden. There is a patio where you can sip an evening wine and look across to the Marlborough hills in the distance. And for a different way to travel round the wineries, they can arrange for you to hire transport by horse and cart.

CRAGLEE LODGE

Bay of Many Coves, Queen Charlotte Sound
Private Bag 407, Picton
phone (03) 579 9223
fax (03) 579 9923
email: craglee@xtra.co.nz

$$$

The Marlborough Sounds must be one of the most beautiful waterways in the world. Craglee was built in 1991 to take full advantage of the native bush and the wonderful view from its site high above the Bay of Many Coves. It can be accessed from the Queen Charlotte Walkway or by boat, but not by road. Truly a chance to get away from it all! There's a spa pool to relax in, perhaps after a bush walk in the area, and fishing, kayaking and 'messing about in boats' can all be arranged.

Framingham Wine Company —

If you're fond of a riesling, look for the Framingham winery. This is their specialty wine and it is made in three styles, from dry through medium/dry to Late Harvest. And they are all delicious! Here is another example of contract grape suppliers turned winemakers. Framingham began in 1981, but it was not until 1994 that they produced the first vintage under their own label. As well as riesling, Framingham now produces a range of both red and white wines, including a méthode traditionelle.

☛ **Conders Bend Road, Renwick**

Phone: (03) 572 8884

Fax: (03) 572 9884

Email: framwine@voyager.co.nz

Hours: for tasting and purchasing, summer 10am-5pm daily, winter 11am-4pm daily.

Eating/other facilities: catering for groups available by arrangement. Tours by arrangement.

Owners: Private company

Winemaker: Anthony Mackenzie

Wines produced

○ Framingham Chardonnay, $20-23
Framingham Gewürztraminer, $16-18
Framingham Méthode Traditionelle, $28-32
Framingham Classic Riesling, $15-18
Framingham Dry Riesling, $18-20
Framingham Late Harvest Riesling, $25-28
Framingham Pinot Gris, $17-19
Framingham Sauvignon Blanc, $15-17

● Framingham Merlot, $22-25
Framingham Syrah, $20-22

Fromm Winery

The Marlborough region was catapulted to world recognition as the producer of distinctive and different sauvignon blancs. Perhaps for that reason people have tended to pay less attention to the reds produced in the region. George Fromm thinks differently. He believes Marlborough reds offer great opportunity provided the vines are treated in the right way. His way is to use organic methods of growing, and to have close-planted vines and hand-picked grapes. The winemaker at Fromm, Hatsch Kalberer, believes that good crop management is essential if you're going to produce good wines. And they've certainly got something right – the La Strada Reserve Pinot Noir has been described by Bob Campbell (MW) as 'outstanding … and one of the country's best'.

☞ **Godfrey Road, Blenheim**

Phone: (03) 572 9355

Fax: (03) 572 9366

Hours: mid-December to end of February, Tuesday to Saturday 11am-5pm; March to mid-December, Saturday only 11am-5pm.

Eating/other facilities: none.

Owners: George and Ruth Fromm

Winemaker: Hatsch Kalberer

Wines produced

○ La Strada Chardonnay, $25-28
  La Strada Chardonnay Reserve, $34-38
  La Strada Gewürztraminer, $25-28
  La Strada Riesling, $24-26
  La Strada Riesling Auslese 375ml, $20-23
  La Strada Riesling Dry, $20-22

● La Strada Malbec Reserve, $36-40
  La Strada Merlot, $18-20
  La Strada Merlot Reserve, $34-38

CRANBROOK COTTAGE

Giffords Road, Rapaura, Blenheim
phone (03) 572 8606
mobile (025) 352 354
fax (03) 572 8707

$$$

This delightful cottage is in the heart of the vineyards. It's been refurbished to make it very comfortable while maintaining its historic charms. Ian and Keren Mitchell's own home – made of mud block and equally charming – is set far enough away to guarantee privacy but close enough if you need assistance. A 'white linen tablecloth' breakfast is brought fresh to you each morning.

HOTEL D'URVILLE

52 Queen Street, Blenheim
PO Box 977, Blenheim
phone (03) 577 9945
fax (03) 577 9946
email:
hoteldurville@clear.net.nz
website: www.durville.co.nz

$$$

The French navigator Jules
Sebastien César Dumont
d'Urville sailed to New
Zealand three times between
1824 and 1840 and he's well
commemorated in this
region. Visitors will come
across his name in many
places, from d'Urville Island
to the east of Tasman Bay to
d'Urville River which flows
into Lake Rotoroa. And, of
course, at this charming
boutique hotel in central
Blenheim. What was the
Public Trust Building in the
1920s was re-opened in 1996
as a nine-room hotel. Its lofty
ceilings and polished floors
give it an air of elegance and
each of the rooms has a four
poster bed and an eclectic
mix of fabrics and antiques.
The in-house restaurant has
an excellent reputation and
makes a point of serving the
gourmet produce and fine
wines of Marlborough.

La Strada Pinot Noir, $28-32
La Strada Pinot Noir Fromm Vineyard, $42-48
La Strada Syrah, $19-22
La Strada Syrah Reserve, $36-39

Gillan Estate Wines ——————

'An elite sparkling wine in New Zealand.' That's the kind
of rave notice that winemakers strive for, and it has been
applied to Toni and Terry Gillan's Vintage Brut Reserve.
This méthode traditionelle is their flagship wine. Its
elegance and complexity have developed over a minimum
of three years' slow maturation on its lees. This takes place
in the temperature-controlled environment of their cellar.
And this is no ordinary cellar! The simple white building
is sympathetic to Marlborough, but also has a flavour of
the Mediterranean – the cellar is in fact the ground floor of
the Gillan's home and is the tasting area   for their winery.
It has a vaulted ceiling and is candlelit for special
occasions. Visitors can also enjoy a champagne brunch
here.

Gillan Estate is a place to linger. You can play petanque
or relax over a picnic under the cherry trees in the garden.
If you're feeling even mildly energetic you can go into the
orchard and pick cherries in season – fresh off the tree and
warmed by the sun these are just heaven! Liqueur cherry
chocolates and desserts can also be bought at the cellar
door.

☛ **Rapaura Road, Blenheim**

Phone: (03) 572 9979

Fax: (03) 572 9980

Email: gillanwines@voyager.co.nz

Hours: for tasting and buying wines, October-June
10am-5pm daily.

Eating/other facilities: restaurant provides

Michael Allan,
winemaker,
Huia Vineyards,
Marlborough

Gillan Estate Wines, Marlborough

CELLAR DOOR

Isabel Estate Vineyard, Marlborough

Framingham Wine Co., Marlborough

Lawsons Vineyard, Marlborough
ABOVE: Barbara and Ross Lawson with Mike Just (left)
BELOW: Harvesting gewürztraminer in the home block

Waipara Springs Wines, Waipara

Weka Pass Railway,
Waipara

Mediterranean-style dining inside and out, and caters to wedding receptions, winemakers' dinners and special functions.

Owners: Terry and Toni Gillan

Winemaker: Sam Weaver

Wines produced

○ Gillan Chardonnay, $18-21
Gillan Sauvignon Blanc, $15-18
Gillan Vintage Brut Reserve (méthode traditionelle) $28-32

● Gillan Merlot, $19-21

Grove Mill Wine Company ____

Grove Mill winery can be found just off State Highway 63 as you come out of Renwick on the way to Nelson. It started off very much entwined with a piece of Blenheim brewing history. The winery's original premises were in the Old Malt House of the former Wairau Brewery founded in 1858. Terry and Toni Gillan (Gillan Estate Wines) were among the founding shareholders of the company and very involved with its start-up. With winemaker David Pearce, they converted the malt house into a winery and restaurant. Subsequently the Gillans set up their own winery, and Grove Mill moved to its present site. Two of their wines are now regarded as classics: the Marlborough Sauvignon Blanc and the Marlborough Riesling. And if you like a gewürztraminer with attitude, try Grove Mill's. Opening off the tasting room is a 'vine library'. Each of the varietals of grape used in the wine production has a vine planted in the 'library' and visitors are welcome to look at and taste the grapes as they sip a little of the wine. And if you've ever doubted wine writers when they say a wine has cut grass, gooseberries, citrus or lychees on the nose – here's a chance to find out what they're on about. Grove

MAXWELL HOUSE

82 Maxwell Road, Blenheim
phone/fax (03) 577 7545
mobile (025) 234 9977

$$

This bed and breakfast is 10 minutes' walk from the centre of Blenheim. What was a grand old Victorian home built in the late 1800s has been restored and includes two large guest rooms, each with their own lounge area. You can have breakfast in your room, on the verandah or at the original 1880s kauri dining table.

THE OLD ST MARY'S CONVENT

Rapaura Road, Blenheim
phone/fax (03) 570 5700
email: oldstmary@xtra.co.nz

$$$

The Sisters of Mercy had this convent built for them in 1901 next to St Mary's Church in Blenheim. Native timbers such as matai, rimu and kauri were used extensively in its construction, creating a building of tremendous charm and character. None of this has been lost in its later history, despite being moved in five pieces to its present location in Rapaura Road. Mieke and Wilfried Holtrop bought the building in 1994 and relocated it to eight hectares in the heart of Marlborough's wine country. Four luxury suites have been created on the first floor. Each has access onto the balcony, which has spectacular views over the surrounding countryside.

Mill's tasting room hosts 'aroma demonstrations' during the weekend and also serves as an art gallery, with changing exhibitions, often from leading New Zealand artists.

☞ **Cnr Waihopi Valley Road and State Highway 63**
Phone: (03) 572 8200
Fax: (03) 572 8211
Email: info@grovemill.co.nz
Hours: 11am to 5pm daily.
Eating/other facilities: art gallery and vine library.
Owners: shareholders
Winemaker: David Pearce

Wines produced

○ Grove Mill Landsdowne Chardonnay, $30-33
Grove Mill Marlborough Chardonnay, $20-22
Grove Mill Sanctuary Chardonnay, $13-15
Grove Mill Pinot Gris, $22-24
Grove Mill Riesling, $17-19
Grove Mill Sanctuary Riesling, $12-13
Grove Mill Sauvignon Blanc, $18-20
Grove Mill Sanctuary Sauvignon Blanc, $13-15

● Grove Mill Pinot Noir, $28-32
Grove Mill Sanctuary Pinotage, $13-15

Hawkesbridge Wines and Estates

A weekend at the Marlborough Wine and Food Festival was the start of this new venture for Mike Veal and his wife Judy. In the local newspaper Mike saw that a block of 16 hectares of land was up for sale. This was definitely an example of 'impulse buying', and within days the deal was done. Now the vineyard is fully planted. Their first vintage was in 1998. Mike uses half his fruit for the Hawkesbridge wines and sells the rest to other producers.

☞ **Hawkesbury Road, Renwick**

Phone: (03) 572 8024

Fax: (03) 572 9489

Email: hawkesbridge@xtra.co.nz

Hours: Christmas to Easter 10.30am-4.30pm or by appointment.

Eating/other facilities: none.

Owners: Mike and Judy Veal

Winemaker: Mike Veal

Wines produced

○ Hawkesbridge Sophie's Vineyard Chardonnay, $18-20

Hawkesbridge Sophie's Vineyard Reserve Chardonnay, $24-27

Hawkesbridge Willowbank Vineyard Sauvignon Blanc, $18-20

● Hawkesbridge Merlot, $25-28

Hawkesbridge Pinot Noir, $24-27

Huia Vineyards

The native bird the huia became extinct in 1907 because of the depletion of the native forests and over-zealous specimen collection for overseas museums. In Maori tradition the white-tipped tail feathers of the huia were greatly prized and used for the adornment of chiefs. The symbolism of the bird's name presents a challenge for the winery to live up to! It certainly is the goal of winemakers Mike and Claire Allan to make high quality, individualistic wines.

PUNGA COVE RESORT

Endeavour Inlet, Queen Charlotte Sound

Rural Bag 408, Picton

freephone 0800 809 697

phone (03) 579 8561

fax (03) 579 8080

email: enquiries@pungacove.co.nz

website: www.pungacove.co.nz

$$-$$$

In 1999 Punga Cove Resort picked up two tourism awards – Mid Range Accommodation and Marlborough Overall Winner. They offer both luxury chalets and studio or self-contained family units. All of them nestle in the bush and have balconies giving privacy and superb views across the water. From Picton, the resort is two hours by car or 90 minutes by water taxi. It's also accessible by helicopter. The restaurant serves gourmet cuisine and Marlborough's excellent wines. And what better place from which to explore the Queen Charlotte Track or do some deep sea fishing? Or just laze about and take in the birdlife and native bush?

The Allans bought their Rapaura property in late 1990, after working in a number of wineries in Marlborough. They had both studied at Roseworthy College in South Australia and also spent time in France. Before that Claire had been involved in restaurants in both New Zealand and Britain. Her interest in food was superseded by a passion for wine, and she and Mike became the winemaking team at Lawson's Dry Hills in Marlborough until late 1996.

Now they're concentrating on their own vineyard. The gewürztraminer has done very well and the chardonnay and riesling have received very favourable mention. Their most recent 'first' is the Huia Méthode Traditionelle.

☛ **Boyces Road, Rapaura, Blenheim**

Phone: (03) 572 8326

Fax: (03) 572 8331

Email: huia.vineyards@xtra.co.nz

Hours: Monday-Saturday 10am-4.30pm.

Eating/other facilities: none.

Owners and winemakers: Michael and Claire Allan

Wines produced

○ Huia Chardonnay, $23-25
Huia Gewürztraminer, $19-21
Huia Méthode Traditionelle, $30-33
Huia Pinot Gris, $19-21
Huia Riesling, $18-20
Huia Sauvignon Blanc, $17-19

● Huia Pinot Noir, $28-32

Hunter's Wines _____

In 1992 Jane Hunter was awarded an OBE. Hers is a story of courage and determination and, ultimately, tremendous success. Her husband Ernie started in the industry in

1980 with the intention of growing grapes as a contract supplier, but decided to try his hand as a winemaker. He poured his prodigious energy into the venture, but in 1987 he was killed in a car accident at the age of 38. Not wanting all their hard work to be wasted, Jane took over running the business. It wasn't exactly foreign territory; she comes from a South Australian grapegrowing family and studied viticulture at university. Working with fellow Australian Gary Duke as winemaker, she has given her own prodigious energy with very successful results. The wines are excellent, and three are regarded as classics: a chardonnay, and two sauvignon blancs, one oak aged. Hunter's restaurant is also one of the best in the region.

☞ **Rapaura Road, Blenheim**

Phone: (03) 572 8489

Fax: (03) 572 8457

Email: hunters@voyager.co.nz

Hours: for tasting and purchasing, Monday-Saturday 9am-5pm, Sunday 9.30am-4pm.

Eating/other facilities: Vintners Restaurant is open seven days for lunch and dinner, bookings essential.

Owner: Jane Hunter OBE

Winemaker: Gary Duke

Wines produced

○ Hunter's Breidecker, $11-12
Hunter's Brut, $25-28
Hunter's Chardonnay, $19-21
Hunter's Gewürztraminer, $14-16
Hunter's Riesling, $14-16
Hunter's Late Harvest Riesling, $13-15
Hunter's Sauvignon Blanc, $15-18
Hunter's Oak Aged Sauvignon Blanc $19-22
Hunter's Spring Creek Vineyard Sauvignon/
   Chardonnay, $13-15
Hunter's Estate Dry White, $10-12

TANGLEWOOD

Queen Charlotte Drive,
The Grove, RD1, Picton
phone (03) 574 2080
fax (03) 574 2044
email: tangles@voyager.co.nz.

$

Half way (16 km in either direction) between Picton and Havelock is The Grove and Tanglewood B&B. It has a private, separate guest wing which includes a small kitchen for self-catering. It's a lovely spot, surrounded by native ferns and only a short walk to a swimming beach and jetty. A great base for kayaking, fishing or bush walking.

Hunter's Merlot/Cabernet, $19-22
Hunter's Pinot Noir, $18-21
Hunter's Estate Red, $14-16

THAINSTONE ESTATE

Giffords Road, Blenheim
phone/fax (03) 572 8823

$$-$$$

Thainstone is in the Wairau Valley and offers a special vineyard homestay experience. Jim and Viv Murray bought their vineyard in 1990. They sell most of their fruit to other winemakers but do make a small quantity of sauvignon blanc and chardonnay themselves. Guests can try these and other local wines with the delicious country-style meals.

Isabel Estate Vineyard _____

Isabel Estate wines have a distinctive character and the sauvignon blanc has had some rave reviews. It has been described as 'pungent and penetrating, crammed to the gills with delicious fruit', 'something special' and 'snappy and herbaceous with a zappy signature of lively acidity'. Michael and Robyn Tiller began as contract grapegrowers, but in 1994 began to produce wines under their own label. They say they 'aim to make inspired wines' and to maintain high quality through maintaining total viticultural control in their vineyards. They restrict yield to optimise quality, and their wines are all produced from their own fruit. But wines aren't the only thing to enjoy at Isabel Estate. Moose Lodge with its very modestly priced accommodation is right there in the vineyard. The winery continues to expand, and Michael and Robyn have a café and underground cellar facilities under way.

☞ **Hawkesbury Road, Renwick**

Phone: (03) 572 8300

Fax: (03) 572 8383

Email: isabel.estate@xtra.co.nz

Hours: for tasting and purchasing, by appointment, preferably between 11am and 4pm.

Eating/other facilities: café and visitor reception facilities. 'Moose Lodge' accommodation in vineyard.

Owners: Michael and Robyn Tiller

Winemaker: Jeff Sinnott

Wines produced

○ Isabel Estate Chardonnay, $26-29
   Isabel Estate Riesling, $19-22
   Isabel Estate Sauvignon Blanc, $22-24
   Isabel Estate Late Harvest Sauvignon Blanc, $23-25

● Isabel Estate Pinot Noir, $32-36

Lawson's Dry Hills _____

Lawson's Dry Hills Sauvignon Blanc has been described as a 'symphony in the glass', their riesling as 'absolutely gorgeous', and the winery as 'regularly producing exemplary wines'. All good reasons to visit, and a very satisfying state of affairs for Ross and Barbara Lawson. They, too, tell the grapegrowers-to-winemakers story. After 12 years as grapegrowers they formed their present company, and the business has grown from processing 15 tonnes of fruit in 1992 to the current 250 tonnes. A remarkable number of their wines have been medal winners. As if that wasn't enough to tempt you down Alabama Road, in summer you can enjoy a vineyard version of fine dining. The restaurant serves such delights as juniper crust wild venison, pan roast scallops, baked salmon fillet and homemade icecream. Barbara says their dinner guests have been known to stroll over to the 'harvest happenings' and taste the juice from the press between courses. Now there's a winery experience! The 'dry hills' are the Wither Hills that fringe the southern side of Blenheim.

☛ **Alabama Road, Blenheim**
   Phone: (03) 578 7674
   Fax: (03) 578 7603
   Email: lawsonswines@xtra.co.nz
   Hours: for tasting and purchasing, 10am-5pm seven days.

TIRIMOANA HOUSE

*Anakiwa Road, Picton
RD 1 Queen Charlotte
Sounds, Marlborough
phone (03) 574 2627
fax (03) 574 2647*

$

Peter and Robyn Churchill have a waterfront house overlooking Okiwa Bay and the start/finish of the Queen Charlotte Walkway. They offer both homestay and self-contained facilities and invite visitors to 'come and share a slice of heaven'. They have an extensive sundeck and a fernery-surrounded spa pool if you just want to laze and relax, or you're welcome to join them in bush walks, fishing or golf. Peter and Robyn are also happy to help make any other arrangements for your enjoyment of the region.

UNO PIU

75 Murphy's Road, Blenheim
phone/fax (03) 578 2235
mobile (025) 241 4493
email: unopiu@iname.com

$$–$$$

Gino and Heather Rocco own Uno Piu and offer a luxurious homestay – a swimming pool enclosed with roses, a sauna, a spa pool, a baby grand piano in the lounge and a welcoming open fire. And you get all this plus Italian hospitality and Gino's homemade pasta. There are three bedrooms available for guests and this lovely old renovated home is set in two hectares, where horses and sheep graze.

Eating/other facilities: fine dining restaurant in the evenings throughout summer.

Owners: Ross and Barbara Lawson

Winemaker: Mike Just

Wines produced

○ Lawson's Dry Hills Chardonnay, $22-24
Lawson's Dry Hills Gewürztraminer, $17-19
Lawson's Dry Hills Riesling, $15-18
Lawson's Dry Hills Sauvignon Blanc, $16-19

● Lawson's Dry Hills Pinot Noir, $23-26

Le Brun Family Estate Winery

This is a return to an old dream for the Le Brun family. Daniel Le Brun has always wanted to make only méthode champenoise and this strictly family venture allows him to do it. He has made a great contribution to New Zealand 'bubbles' but with the expansion of Cellier Le Brun got drawn into making other lines. Now he is producing only a non-vintage Blanc de Blancs. Released to be enjoyed at the start of the new millennium, Daniel No. 1 has come out to glowing reviews. Through this winery Daniel also processes and produces méthode champenoise for other winemakers. The Le Bruns have opened a small wine shop for their own wine and all those bits and pieces that complement bubbles – like caviar!

☞ **Rapaura Rd, Blenheim**

Phone: (03) 572 9876

Fax: (03) 572 9857

Email: lbfe@voyager.co.nz

Hours for tasting and purchasing: summer seven days 9.30am-5pm. Reduced hours over winter.

Eating/other facilities: none.

Owner: The Le Brun family

Winemaker: Daniel Le Brun

Wines produced

○ Daniel No. 1, $32-35

Montana Wines Marlborough —

It was Montana Wines that made the leap of faith in the region's potential. In 1973 the company planted the first commercial vineyards with sauvignon blanc and changed the face of Marlborough for ever. The company has its head office in Auckland, but owns vineyards in Hawke's Bay and Gisborne as well as Marlborough.

Montana is New Zealand's largest wine producer and was founded by Ivan Yukich, a Dalmatian who settled in New Zealand in 1934. The company makes good wines at all price levels, differentiating them in the market with different labels. The Marlborough winery specialises in méthode traditionelle and is home to Deutz Marlborough Cuvée, which in 1998 won 'Sparkling Wine of the Year' at the International Wine Challenge in London. That and the Deutz Marlborough Blanc de Blancs are regarded as classic wines.

Montana has plans for a multi-million-dollar wine tourism complex at Brancott Estate. As well as the usual retail facilities, there will be a restaurant and courtyard for dining, where the emphasis will be on fresh local produce. The complex will include a tasting room and an area devoted to wine education. Montana's architects promise a building that 'combines a distinctly vernacular New Zealand style of architecture with the more traditional rural French style often associated with wine'.

☞ **Main South Highway, Blenheim**
   Phone: (03) 578 2099

WAIHOPI HEIGHTS

1087 Waihopi Valley Road,
Blenheim
Tummil Flat, RD 6, Blenheim
phone (03) 572 4018
fax (03) 572 4118.

$$$

You could treat yourself to a stay at Waihopi Heights after tackling one of the Ramshead Tracks around Mount Horrible! The hill on which the house is built gives extensive views across the valley. It's been designed to make the most of the region's sunny climate so you can enjoy breakfast or a barbecue outdoors. It's an ideal place from which to make the most of this lovely wine region, but sometimes it's nice to be able to relax in one spot. Here visitors can swim in the pool or play petanque or table tennis.

57

WAIKAWA BAY HOMESTAY

*Waikawa Bay is three
kilometres from Picton. Hosts
Yvonne and Gary Roberts will
give precise instructions on
how to get there.*
Phone/fax (03) 573 8965

$-$$

In their roomy colonial
cottage Yvonne and Gary
have two guest bedrooms.
They describe themselves as
'young middle-aged and
recently escaped from big
city corporate life'. They like
fine food and wines, good
music, good books and good
conversation. They also love
to share this lovely part of
New Zealand with visitors.

Fax: (03) 578 0463

Hours: for tasting and purchasing, Monday-Saturday
9am-5pm, Sunday 11am-4pm. Winery tours on the
hour 10am-3pm Monday-Saturday. Bookings
essential.

Eating/other facilities: a wine tourism complex
with restaurant and courtyard dining is currently in
the planning stage.

Owners: Corporate Investment Ltd

Chief winemaker: Jeff Clarke

Wines produced

○ Deutz Marlborough Cuvée Blanc de Blancs, $34-36
Deutz Marlborough Cuvée Brut, $27-29
Deutz Marlborough Pinot Noir Cuvée, $37-40
Montana Reserve Barrique Matured Chardonnay,
$20-22
Montana Marlborough Chardonnay, $14-16
Renwick Estate Chardonnay, $24-26
Montana Late Harvest Selection 375ml, $13-15
Montana Reserve Vintage Release Riesling, $17-19
Saints Marlborough Noble Riesling 375ml, $16-19
Montana Marlborough Riesling, $13-14
Brancott Estate Sauvignon Blanc, $25-27
Montana Reserve Vineyard Selection Sauvignon
Blanc, $17-19
Montana Marlborough Sauvignon Blanc, $13-15

● Fairhall Estate Cabernet Sauvignon Merlot, $32-35
Montana Reserve Barrique Matured Merlot, $20-22
Montana Reserve Barrique Matured Pinot Noir,
$35-38
Saints Marlborough Pinot Noir, $19-22

Mud House Wine Company ——

John and Jennifer Joslin have gone out and done the sort of things many of us only dream about. For six years they cruised the world in their yacht *Dancing Wave*. Then they found Marlborough and decided to stay. They bought their land in 1992 and named it Le Grys Vineyard (Jennifer's family name). On this land they built an unusual and beautiful mud-block house, which also has some homestay accommodation. The word soon spread about the comforts of their homestay and demand increased, which encouraged them to build a separate cottage in the same mud-block style as their house. 'Waterfall Lodge' has great views of the Richmond Range and of the vineyard. Breakfast comes in a hamper delivered to the door. Bliss!

HIGH COUNTRY HORSE TREKS

Ardnadam, Taylor Pass Road, Redwood Village, Blenheim

phone/fax (03) 577 9424

Whether you're a beginner or an experienced rider, this company promises you a well-trained and user-friendly horse! They offer seven different rides through the picturesque back country and take groups of up to 10 people.

☛ **Conders Bend Road, Renwick**

   Phone: (03) 572 9490

   Fax: (03) 572 9491

   Email: legrys@voyager.co.nz

   Hours: 10am-5pm.

   Eating/other facilities: mud-block cottage in vineyard.

   Owners: John and Jennifer Joslin

   Winemaker: Matt Thomson

Wines produced

○ Le Grys Marlborough Chardonnay, $20-22
   Mud House Marlborough Chardonnay, $20-22
   Le Grys Marlborough Sauvignon Blanc, $16-18
   Mud House Marlborough Sauvignon Blanc, $16-18

● Mud House Marlborough Merlot, $28-30
   Mud House Marlborough Pinot Noir, $31-34

RIVER RAFTING

'Action in Marlborough'
59 Lakings Road, Blenheim
phone/fax (03) 578 4531
freephone 0800 266 266
email: wallyb@clear.net.nz

Rafting is a great way to see the countryside. The company offers day trips on the Gowan River (one of New Zealand's fastest-flowing rivers) and the Buller River, or you can enjoy a multi-day expedition down the Clarence River which will take you through Marlborough's back country.

Omaka Springs Estate _____

Established in 1991, the Omaka Springs vineyard has grown from 4 to 61 hectares in 10 years, which is certainly rapid expansion. And that's only the area planted in grapes. Omaka Springs has another 8 hectares of olives. Olive growing is a fledgling industry in the South Island but it has all the hallmarks of the early wine industry – passionate growers and rapid expansion. At Omaka Springs visitors can buy olives, olive oil and olive trees at the cellar door. It may be the South Pacific but the combination of olives and wine certainly have delightful Mediterranean overtones.

☛ **Kennedy's Road, Blenheim**

Phone: (03) 572 9933

Fax: (03) 572 9934

Email: geoff@clear.net.nz

Hours: 10.30am-4.30pm seven days from October to May. At other times by appointment.

Eating/other facilities: sales of estate-produced extra virgin olive oil, olive plants and walnuts.

Owner: Geoff Jensen

Winemaker: Ian Marchant

Wines produced

○ Omaka Springs Chardonnay, $16-18
Omaka Springs Reserve Chardonnay, $25-28
Omaka Springs Pinot Gris, $13-15
Omaka Springs Riesling, $12-14
Omaka Springs Sauvignon Blanc, $15-17

● Omaka Springs Gamay Noir, $13-15
Omaka Springs Merlot, $18-20
Omaka Springs Reserve Pinot Noir, $25-28

Ponder Estate

Ponder Estate is one of the most attractive in the Marlborough region. Once again there's the wonderful ambience created by the combination of vineyard and olive groves against a backdrop of handsome hills. In 1987 artist Michael Ponder and his wife Dianne lived in Blenheim, and Michael was exhibiting widely in Europe. But he'd always had a yen to farm, and in that year they bought 87 acres (36 hectares) at the mouth of the Brancott Valley.

This 'retirement project' is certainly not easing them into old age! They began as grapegrowers but in 1994 produced the first wine under their own label. That was also the year they achieved the first pressing of extra virgin olive oil from their own olive groves, one of the first to do so in New Zealand. In 1995 they won a gold medal for their sauvignon blanc and in 1996 their olive oil was rated among the top 15 in the world.

The olive side of the business came about because the front paddock of their property wasn't suitable for grapes. It has a stream running through it and the water rises on one side of it, providing natural irrigation for the olive trees. Michael and Dianne originally imported their trees from Israel and went there to learn how to propagate. They've now branched out into having assorted cultivars for sale, along with several varieties of lavender. They have established the Shed Gallery where you can taste and buy their wines, olive oil, olive trees and lavender plants, as well as Michael's artworks. Each year Michael does a new painting for the Ponder Estate label.

☛ **New Renwick Road, Blenheim**
   Phone: (03) 572 8642
   Fax: (03) 572 9034
   Email: ponderestate@xtra.co.nz
   Hours: 10am-4.30pm daily.

WINDHAWK RIVER GUIDES

phone (03) 572 8974
fax (03) 572 9560
email: bod@clear.net.nz

Windhawk River Guides are a company of professional fly-fishing guides. If you've always wanted to learn the art of fly-fishing, this is where to go for classes. They offer day or extended trips. You can travel to your river by 4WD vehicle, on a packhorse or by helicopter. Windhawk are based in the Omaka Valley near Blenheim.

SNAPPER FISHING CHARTERS

PO Box 21, Havelock
phone/fax (03) 574 2911
mobile (025) 397 178
email: scottanderson@
marlborough.gen.nz

There's nothing quite like going out into the beautiful Marlborough Sounds to try your luck with snapper. Scott Anderson's Snapper Fishing Charters are based at Havelock. You can book for a half day or full day, and Scott will take you to Raetihi Lodge in the Kenepuru Sound for a delicious lunch of the best Marlborough food and wine.

Eating/other facilities: Olive Grove and Olive Press House open to the public all year round. Olive tree and lavender nursery. Paintings and prints by Michael Ponder.

Owners: Mike and Di Ponder

Winemaker: Graeme Paul and Alan McCorkindale (consultant)

Wines produced
○ Ponder Estate Chardonnay, $18-21
Ponder Estate Riesling, $18-20
Ponder Estate Sauvignon Blanc, $16-19

● Ponder Estate Pinot Noir, $35-40

Saint Clair Estate Wines _____

This estate has quite an impressive track record. Their first wines were made in 1994, and over the last six years every one of them has won a medal. In 1999 the Omaka Reserve Chardonnay won best in its class and Champion White Wine at the annual Bragato Wine Awards. Interestingly for a New Zealand red wine, their merlot is gaining a good reputation in Europe. The intense fruit flavours of Marlborough is what makes the region's white wines stand out, but Neal Ibbotson believes reds have the potential to be just as interesting. He and his wife Judy were among Marlborough's first private grapegrowers back in 1978. Try their single vineyard Awatere Valley Reserve Sauvignon Blanc or the single vineyard Omaka Reserve Chardonnay.

☞ **739 New Renwick Road, Blenheim**
Phone: (03) 578 8695
Fax: (03) 578 8696
Hours: tasting at 'Country Life' (Aberharts Road,

Grovetown, 1 km north of Blenheim on State Highway 1 to Picton.) Open seven days 10am-4pm, phone/fax: (03) 577 7736.

Eating/other facilities: none.

Owners: Neal and Judy Ibbotson

Winemakers: Kim Crawford and Matt Thomson

Wines produced

○ St Clair Marlborough Chardonnay, $16-18
St Clair Marlborough Unoaked Chardonnay, $14-16
St Clair Omaka Reserve Chardonnay, $22-24
St Clair Marlborough Riesling, $14-16
St Clair Marlborough Noble Botrytis Riesling 375ml, $22-25
St Clair Marlborough Sauvignon Blanc, $14-16
St Clair Awatere Valley Reserve Sauvignon Blanc, $17-20

● St Clair Marlborough Merlot, $17-20
St Clair Rapaura Reserve Merlot, $24-28

SEA KAYAKING ADVENTURE TOURS

Anakiwa Road, Picton
phone/fax (03) 574 2765
mobile (025) 490 365
email: SKATA@xtra.co.nz

This is another magical way to travel the coastline and nip in and out of the many inlets in the Sounds. Sea Kayaking Adventure Tours Anakiwa is based at the end of the Queen Charlotte Track. For experienced kayakers they offer 'freedom hire', but they also provide guided trips through Queen Charlotte Sound and Pelorus and Keneperu Sounds.

Selaks Drylands Estate Winery

Selaks is a long-established Auckland winery, which in 1998 was bought by another major North Island producer, Nobilo Vintners. The Drylands Estate was established in 1994 by Selaks to make all its Marlborough wines – 'good humoured wines', as they put it in their advertisements, and who would want to argue with that. The one to particularly look out for is their classic sauvignon blanc/sémillon.

☞ **Hammerichs Road, Rapaura, Blenheim**
Phone: (03) 570 5252
Fax: (03) 570 5272

63

ECOTOURS DOLPHIN WATCH

PO Box 197, Picton
phone (03) 573 8040
fax (03) 573 7906

A boat cruise is an enjoyable way to see the many seabirds, seals and dolphins of the area. Marlborough is also the home of the Motuara Island Bird Sanctuary, where the Department of Conservation has a number of programmes for the preservation of some of the rarer species. Dolphin Watch Marlborough offers fully guided eco-tours that take you cruising in search of dolphins in the Sounds and to Motuara Island. They will also take you to Ship Cove, an anchorage point for Captain Cook in 1770 on his voyages of exploration. The company is based next door to the railway station in Picton.

Hours: 10am-5pm daily in summer, 10am-4pm Wednesday-Sunday in winter.

Eating/other facilities: none.

Owners: Nobilo Vintners Ltd

Winemaker: Darryl Woolley

Wines produced

○ Selaks Drylands Chardonnay, $16-19

Selaks Premium Selection Marlborough Chardonnay, $15-17

Selaks Drylands Estate Fumé Barrique (sauvignon blanc/sémillon) $16-18

Selaks Drylands Riesling (dry), $16-18

Selaks Premium Selection Marlborough Riesling, $13-15

Selaks Drylands Sauvignon Blanc, $16-18

Selaks Premium Selection Marlborough Sauvignon Blanc, $13-15

Seresin Estate

Seresin Estate was established by Michael Seresin, a New Zealand film maker based in London, who happens to have a passion for wine. He admits he knew nothing about winemaking at the start, but all that changed when he took on Brian Bicknell as his winemaker. Before joining Seresin, Brian's experience included being chief winemaker for Vina Errazuriz in Chile for three years as well as winemaking in Bordeaux.

The vineyards are planted on prime alluvial land, each providing a distinct and different meso-climate. The Seresin philosophy is that agricultural activity should work in harmony with nature and so the vineyard has been landscaped to complement the environment. Native trees have been planted at random round the vineyard and olive trees (Seresin Estate is also involved in producing extra virgin olive oil) line the boundaries of the estate. And if you were wondering about how the hand fits into the design of the label – it's a symbol of strength, the gateway to the heart, the tiller of the soil, and the mark of the artisan.

☞ **Bedford Road, Blenheim**

Phone: (03) 572 9408

Fax: (03) 572 9850

Email: seresin@xtra.co.nz

Hours: Monday-Sunday 10am-4.30pm during summer and Monday-Friday 10am-4.30pm in winter.

Eating/other facilities: none.

Owner: Michael Seresin

Winemaker: Brian Bicknell

Wines produced

○ Seresin Estate Chardonnay, $18-21
Seresin Reserve Chardonnay, $28-32
Seresin Pinot Gris, $23-26
Seresin Sauvignon Blanc, $20-24

● Seresin Pinot Noir, $32-35

THE EDWIN FOX MARITIME CENTRE

phone (03) 573 6868
fax (03) 573 6874
email: edwinfoxsoc@xtra.co.nz.

Built of teak in India in 1853, and still redolent with many an historical tale, the *Edwin Fox* is the last survivor of the sailing ships that brought immigrants to New Zealand. And that's not her only claim to fame – she's also the only surviving Australian convict ship and the only surviving troop transport from the Crimean War. The Edwin Fox Maritime Centre on the Picton waterfront is a fascinating place to visit, and the ship can be seen in the adjacent dock. Open seven days 8.45am-5pm.

Shingle Peak Wines _____

Brothers Bill and Ross Spence built up Matua Valley Wines from small beginnings in the North Island. In 1989 they established their foothold in the South Island. Having pioneered sauvignon blanc in New Zealand, it seems appropriate that they should choose Marlborough for their South Island venture. Their Marlborough wines are made from estate-grown grapes as well as some bought in from local growers. The Shingle Peak Sauvignon Blanc is a truly top quality wine, but don't overlook their others.

MAIL BOAT CRUISE

phone (03) 573 6175
Many of the bays in the
Marlborough Sounds can be
reached only by water, and
there are a number of water
taxis that will drop you off at
the various secluded lodges
in the area. Another great
way to explore, though, is to
join the Mail Boat Cruise. It
goes on Tuesdays, Thursdays
and Fridays, leaving the
Havelock Marina at 9.30am
and the Picton Marina at
10.15am. Each day the boat
takes a different route
through Pelorus Sound.

☛ **Rapaura Road, Blenheim**

Phone: (03) 572 9899

Fax: (03) 572 9889

Email: matua@ihug.co.nz

Hours: tasting and buying daily 10am-5pm at the winery or at Wairau River Wines shop.

Eating/other facilities: none.

Owners: Ross and Bill Spence, Ian and Maureen Margan and Mark Robertson

Winemaker: Mark Robertson

Wines produced

○ Shingle Peak Chardonnay, $19-22
Shingle Peak Méthode Traditionelle, $19-22
Shingle Peak Pinot Gris, $17-20
Shingle Peak Riesling, $14-17
Shingle Peak Sauvignon Blanc, $17-20

Stoneleigh Vineyard ____

Stoneleigh is one of the most successful brands of Corbans and is named after the stony soils evident immediately around this Marlborough winery. In the heat of the day, these stones reflect sunlight onto the vines, speeding the ripening process, while the cool nights maintain intense fruit flavours. Stoneleigh Vineyard is in the midst of multi-million dollar expansions, including vineyard acquisitions (present vineyard coverage is over 180 hectares), a major winery upgrade and the establishment of a 600,000-plant nursery.

Stoneleigh's main focuses are sauvignon blanc, chardonnay and pinot noir, with riesling another important aspect of its production – both for the local and export markets. Stoneleigh Marlborough Riesling is one of the best-value wines in the country and one that wins medals and trophies year in, year out. A must-try when you visit this winery – it ages beautifully too.

☞ **Jacksons Road, Blenheim**

    Phone: (03) 572 8198

    Fax: (03) 572 8199

    Website: www.stoneleigh.co.nz.

    Hours: 10am-4.30 daily, seven days. Tours of the winery may be available by appointment.

    Eating/other facilities: none.

    Owners: Corbans Wines Ltd

    Winemaker: Sam Weaver

Wines produced

○ Stoneleigh Vineyard Marlborough Chardonnay, $16-18

    Stoneleigh Vineyard Marlborough Riesling, $15-17

    Stoneleigh Vineyard Marlborough Sauvignon Blanc, $15-17

● Stoneleigh Vineyard Marlborough Cabernet Sauvignon, $16-18

    Stoneleigh Vineyard Marlborough Pinot Noir, $16-18

Te Whare Ra Wines _____

The present owner of Te Whare Ra is Christine Smith, who bought the winery in 1997 with her husband Roger, who sadly passed away in 1999. The winery dates from the early days of winemaking in Marlborough and has been one of the most individualistic of them all.

Joyce and Allen Hogan, the original owners, planted their first vines in 1979 and built the winery three years later. Te Whare Ra means 'house in the sun', and the winery is built of earth bricks with a timbered exterior.

QUEEN CHARLOTTE TRACK

This is one of the great walks of New Zealand. In 1998 it won the 'Best Visitor Attraction' in the New Zealand Tourism Awards. It winds its way over 67 kilometres from Ship Cove in the outer Queen Charlotte Sound to Anakiwa (home of New Zealand's Outward Bound School). The track goes from sea level to hill saddles from which you can experience the most stunning views of the area. The beautiful native bush is also home to a wide range of native birds. You don't have to walk all 67 kilometres! There are many entry and exit points, and various companies offer water transport and pack transfer. There is also a variety of accommodation along the way.

For further information on the track contact the Picton or Blenheim Information Centres.

BROOKSDALE GARDEN & FARM

Brookby Road, Omaka Valley phone (03) 572 8484

In the Omaka Valley, near Blenheim, you can enjoy not only a lovely garden but also a wide range of unusual birdlife. There are five ponds that are home to black and white swans, Carolina mandarin wood ducks, as well as pheasants and rare species of poultry which have specially built rustic houses. There is also a ginkgo avenue and expansive, colourful plantings. Visits September to March by appointment.

With a sense of history, they sold their wines under the Duke of Marlborough label – he who defeated the French at the Battle of Blenheim in 1704. They named their cabernet-based red wine after Sarah Jennings, the Duke of Marlborough's wife. However it was their botrytised white wines that really excited their fans in the wine world.

☞ **56 Anglesea Street, Renwick**

Phone: (03) 572 8581

Fax: (03) 572 8518

Email: rogersmith@xtra.co.nz

Hours: daily 10.30am-4.30pm in summer. Winter more variable. Phone to check hours between Easter and Labour weekend.

Eating/other facilities: none.

Owner: Christine Smith

Winemaker: Warwick Foley

Wines produced

○ Te Whare Ra Berry Selection 375ml, $23-25

Te Whare Ra Duke Of Marlborough Chardonnay (oaked), $18-20

Te Whare Ra Duke of Marlborough Chardonnay (unoaked), $17-19

Te Whare Ra Duke of Marlborough Gewürztraminer, $20-23

Te Whare Ra Dry Gewürztraminer, $12-14

Te Whare Ra Starfish Cove Gewürztraminer, $14-16

Te Whare Ra Duke of Marlborough Riesling, $16-18

Te Whare Ra Riesling, $16-18

Te Whare Ra Starfish Cove Riesling, $14-16

Te Whare Ra Sémillon, $18-20

● Te Whare Ra Sarah Jennings (Cabernet Sauvignon/ Cabernet Franc/Merlot), $22-25

Terrace Road ———————————
(*See* Cellier Le Brun)

Vavasour Wines Ltd ——————

The wines that come from the Awatere Valley, south of Blenheim, have quite distinctive characteristics, and Vavasour Wines was one of the earliest to appreciate their potential. Since the 1890s the property had been a sheep and beef farm owned by the Vavasour family. It was Peter Vavasour who, along with viticulturist Richard Bowling, saw the potential for wine production. In 1986 a company was formed, and the winery was built in 1988 on the terraces bordering the Awatere River. It's a spectacular site with the sea to the north and Mt Tapuaenuku to the south. (Tapuaenuku means 'the footsteps of the rainbow god'.) Although they no longer enter their wines in competitions, in past years they have won many awards. Vavasour Chardonnay and Sauvignon Blanc are both regarded as classic wines. The winery's premium wines all carry the Vavasour label and are made from grapes grown in the Awatere Valley. The Dashwood label indicates wines made for early drinking, and these are made from grapes either from Awatere Valley or Wairau Valley.

☛ **Redwood Pass Road, Awatere Valley (4km from State Highway 1)**

Phone: (03) 575 7481

Fax: (03) 575 7240

Hours: daily 10am-5pm during summer, Monday-Saturday in winter.

Eating/other facilities: none, but visitors are welcome to bring a picnic and enjoy the gardens.

Owners: shareholders

Winemaker: Glenn Thomas

CRUISING THE SOUNDS

Affinity Charters
Havelock Marina
phone (03) 574 2180
fax (03) 574 2160

Affinity Charters, based in Havelock, specialises in live-aboard cruises around the Marlborough Sounds. The vessel has eight private cabins and you can take two, three or five-day cruises. A number of the cruises are designed to cater for special interests: gardens, sites of historical interest, fishing and diving or a gourmet trip that will take you to marine farms and allow you to sample some of the region's wines.

Wines produced

○ Dashwood Chardonnay, $14-16
Vavasour Chardonnay, $19-21
Vavasour Riesling, $18-20
Dashwood Sauvignon Blanc, $13-15
Vavasour Sauvignon Blanc, $18-20

● Dashwood Cabernet Sauvignon, $15-17
Vavasour Cabernet Sauvignon, $19-22

Villa Maria Estate

Villa Maria, which has long been a highly successful Auckland company, wasn't slow to recognise the quality of the fruit to come out of Marlborough. For some time it has bought grapes from contract growers in the region. Now it has big plans for its presence in Marlborough and the company's goal is to produce wines of exceptional quality. And they're well on their way, with the 1998 Reserve Marlborough Chardonnay taking the Champion Chardonnay and Reserve Wine of the Show at the 1999 Air New Zealand Wine Awards. The first stage of a $7.5m Marlborough winery complex is complete and in the early stages will be used to produce white wines. The complex was three years in the planning and Villa Maria say it will be their flagship winery when it is complete. The wine shop opened at the start of the summer season in 1999 and offers a wide range of Villa Maria wines.

☛ **Cnr Paynters Road and New Renwick Road, Blenheim**

Phone: (03) 577 9530

Fax: (03) 577 9585

Email: craigm@villa.co.nz

Hours: winery shop open 10am-5pm Monday-Saturday. Tours of the winery by appointment.

Eating/other facilities: none.

Owner: Villa Maria Estate Ltd

Winemakers: Michelle Richardson, George Geris (assistant)

Wines produced

○ Villa Maria Reserve Chardonnay, $24-27
Villa Maria Cellar Selection Chardonnay, $18-21
Villa Maria Private Bin Gewürztraminer, $14-16
Villa Maria Reserve Noble Riesling 375ml, $39-42
Villa Maria Private Bin Riesling, $14-16
Villa Maria Cellar Selection Late Harvest Riesling 375ml, $15-17
Villa Maria Reserve Clifford Bay Sauvignon Blanc, $21-24
Villa Maria Private Bin Sauvignon Blanc, $14-16
Villa Maria Cellar Selection Sauvignon Blanc, $18-21

● Villa Maria Reserve Syrah, $23-26

Wairau River Wines _____

In a region where there's plenty of competition, Wairau River Wines, established in 1989, make a highly regarded sauvignon blanc. It's rich and lush and worth looking out for. And there's no better place to taste it than Wairau River Wines cellar and restaurant.

Built of mud blocks, it's cosy and welcoming in winter and in summer offers cool relief from the Marlborough sunshine. You can also sit and sip at tables outside and enjoy the spectacular view across the vineyard to the hills beyond. The food is delicious and the menu offers many local gourmet delights.

Chris and Phil Rose were pioneers in the Rapaura district. They have extensive vineyards over three sites, and in fact sell a considerable proportion of their fruit to

LAVENDER WALK

State Highway 63,
Wairau Valley
phone (03) 572 2851
fax (03) 572 2841

Tucked into the Wairau Valley is Leighvander Cottage where you can experience the old-fashioned but enduring delights of the lavender flower. You can stroll along a lavender walk and buy plants for the garden at home – the cottage's garden studio has a wide range of lavender products for sale. They've all been made in Marlborough, using the oil produced at Leighvander. Open seven days 10am-4.30pm from 1 November to 30 April or by appointment.

THE RAMSHEAD WALKING TRACKS

Tyntesfield Road, Waihopai Valley (32 km from Blenheim) phone (03) 572 4016 fax (03) 572 4046 email: ramshead@voyager.co.nz website: www.voyager.co.nz/ ~ramshead/

Having glimpsed the beauty of Marlborough's rugged high country from the comfort of your favourite vineyard, you could be tempted to explore a bit more! The Ramshead is truly 'heading for the hills'. It's merino territory and until recently these tracks and ranges were rarely travelled by people other than sheep musterers. Now you can choose anything from a one to four-day walk in the wild and rocky country around Mount Horrible. The Ramshead Walking Tracks will get you to Cloudy Bay, past Mistake Creek or along the challenging Long Arm. They will take you through beech forests and to heights from where you can see across Marlborough to the Sounds and, on a clear day, as far as the North Island.

other wine producers. They don't make a wide range of wines themselves, but what they do make is very good. When vintage conditions make it possible, Wairau River Wines make a delicious botrytised riesling.

☞ **Cnr Rapaura Road and State Highway 6, Blenheim**

Phone: (03) 572 8584 (hm) (03) 572 9800 (wk)

Fax: (03) 572 9885

Hours: for tasting and purchasing, 10am-5pm seven days.

Eating/other facilities: restaurant open 10am-5pm seven days, and also available for special functions.

Owners: Phil and Chris Rose

Winemaker: John Belsham

Wines produced

○ Wairau River Chardonnay, $21-23
Wairau River Dry Riesling, $16-18
Wairau River Late Harvest Botrytised Riesling 375ml, $30-33
Wairau River Reserve Botrytised Riesling 375ml, $40-43
Wairau River Sauvignon Blanc, $17-19
Wairau River Reserve Sauvignon Blanc, $22-24

Whitehaven Wine Company ——

Sue and Greg White, with winemaker Simon Waghorn, do things a little differently. They source fruit from 14 vineyards in Marlborough's Wairau and Awatere Valleys and pour their energies and expertise into producing good wines. The winery was established in 1994 and quickly gained a reputation for producing quality wines, including the Whitehaven Marlborough Sauvignon Blanc, which is regarded as a classic. In a relatively short time they have considerably expanded their production and now export around the world.

☛ 1 Dodson Street, Blenheim

Phone: (03) 577 8861

Fax: (03) 577 8868

Email: whitehaven@xtra.co.nz

Hours: for tasting and purchasing, daily 10am-4pm.

Eating/other facilities: Whitehaven Café open daily from 10am, providing all day dining, including evenings.

Owners: Greg and Sue White and Simon Waghorn

Winemaker: Simon Waghorn

(cont'd)
You can freedom walk or have a guide and there's backpacker accommodation on the way. The tracks are open September to March and bookings need to be made for all except the one-day walks.

Wines produced

○ Whitehaven Chardonnay, $17-19
Whitehaven Chardonnay Mendoza, $21-23
Whitehaven Single Vineyard Reserve
    Gewürztraminer, $19-21
Whitehaven Single Vineyard Reserve Pinot Gris,
    $19-21
Whitehaven Riesling, $15-17
Whitehaven Single Vineyard Reserve Riesling,
    $19-21
Whitehaven Single Vineyard Reserve Noble Riesling
    375ml, $19-22
Whitehaven Sauvignon Blanc, $16-18
Whitehaven Barrel Fermented Sauvignon Blanc,
    $19-21
Whitehaven Single Vineyard Reserve Sauvignon
    Blanc, $19-22

● Whitehaven Pinot Noir, $23-26

waipara

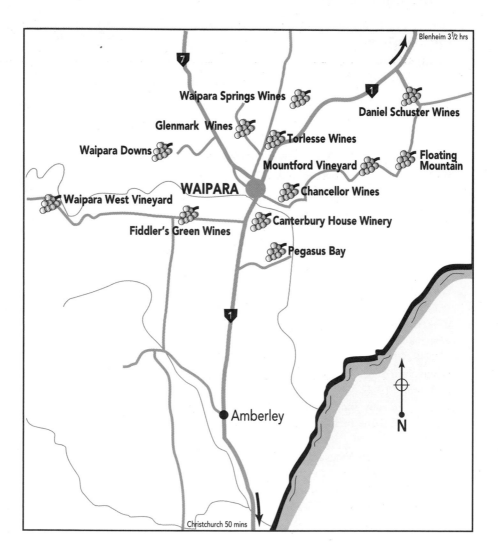

Waipara Springs Wines

Glenmark Wines

Waipara Downs

Daniel Schuster Wines

Torlesse Wines

Mountford Vineyard

Floating Mountain

WAIPARA

Waipara West Vineyard

Chancellor Wines

Fiddler's Green Wines

Canterbury House Winery

Pegasus Bay

Blenheim 3½ hrs

Amberley

N

Christchurch 50 mins

The Waipara Valley in North Canterbury is one of the most promising grapegrowing areas of New Zealand for pinot noir. It has some ideal viticultural conditions – a warm dry climate and limestone-rich soils. Many of the vineyards are protected from the cool easterly breezes typical of this region by its eastern hills, allowing mesoclimates with consistently high summer temperatures. Combined with long, sunny autumns, these conditions often produce intensely flavoured ripe grapes. But it was only around 1980 that the first commercial plantings of grapes were made. Now Waipara Valley has more than 25 grapegrowers and 12 wine producers. And they're on the increase.

Many of the winemakers also have small cafés or restaurants attached to their wineries. Set in the gentle, rolling hills of the area, they're a delight to visit. In March each year the region hosts a very popular wine and food celebration at the Glenmark Church.

The growing number of wineries is reason enough to make the short journey from Christchurch to this lovely area but, as they say, there's more! Traditionally this is a farming area, and quite a number of farmstays are on offer for visitors. The valley is an excellent base for exploring the surrounding Hurunui district. This stretches from the northernmost point of the Southern Alps – Lewis Pass – to the Pacific Ocean. You can enjoy the mountain air and beautiful beech forests of the Lewis; luxuriate in the hot springs of Hanmer village, travel on a vintage steam train through the Weka Pass, fish in the lakes and rivers of the region, go whale watching off the Kaikoura coast or relax on the beach at Gore Bay.

All this and excellent wine, too!

REGIONAL HIGHLIGHTS

WAIPARA WINE AND FOOD CELEBRATION

March, the time of the grape harvest, is also the time for this popular festival, which is held at the Glenmark Church.

KAIKOURA SEAFEST

In the first weekend of October Kaikoura celebrates the abundance of the ocean at this seafest, which has become a great favourite. The name Kaikoura means 'to eat crayfish'.

AUTHOR'S FAVOURITES

Canterbury House Sauvignon Blanc

Pegasus Bay Pinot Noir

Pegasus Bay Riesling

Waipara Springs Barrique Chardonnay

Waipara Springs Riesling

Hanmer Springs
Amuri Drive, Hanmer
Private Bag, Amuri Drive
Freephone 0800 733 426
phone (03) 315 7128
fax (03) 315 7658
email: hanvin@nzhost.co.nz

Kaikoura
Westend, Kaikoura
phone (03) 319 5641
fax (03) 319 6819
email: info@kaikoura.co.nz

the wineries

Canterbury House Winery

The first vineyards of this relatively new winery were planted in 1994. In 1999, their 1998 sauvignon blanc took gold and the overall winner's trophy in the Royal Easter Show Wine Awards. And when you taste it you'll understand why!

Waipara worked its magic on Michael Reid and his wife, who were taking a holiday in New Zealand. From California, they had long been interested in wine, and decided to turn their hobby into their business. The couple has built a magnificent winery by the main highway. It's certainly an eye-catching building and it will beckon you in for some tasting. In these almost baronial surroundings you can accompany your wine with stylish snacks or have a full lunch.

All Canterbury House wines are made from estate-grown grapes, a policy that Michael sees as essential to control quality. But there are no plans to keep this as a boutique winery – the business will expand over time, but the focus will remain on producing premium estate wines.

The Reids are justifiably proud of the sauvignon blanc, but feel that pinot noir will be the flagship of the estate because the area is ideal for this grape and winemaker

THE CRAYPOT CAFÉ & BAR

70 Westend, Kaikoura
phone (03) 319 6027

Not surprisingly, given the fact that Kaikoura means 'to eat crayfish', the Craypot specialises in crayfish and other seafood, straight from the nearby ocean. It's in the heart of town, fully licensed and has a very pleasant atmosphere.

THE GARDEN HOUSE CAFÉ

Thermal Reserve, Hanmer, phone (03) 315 7115

Work up an appetite walking through the forest to the top of Conical Hill (about one hour return). The summit is at 550 metres and has the most magnificent views of this attractive alpine region. The café is within the hot springs reserve of Hanmer village, so when you return from your walk you can have a soak in a hot pool and contemplate the pleasures of lunch.

HISLOP'S WHOLEFOODS CAFÉ

33 Beach Rd, Kaikoura phone (03) 319 6971

With its wonderful location on Beach Road, this café provides a visual treat as well as excellent food. Where possible, Hislop's uses organically grown ingredients. The food is always fresh and very tasty.

Mark Rattray has a strong reputation in the production of this wine. The 1998 pinot noir took a silver at the Concours Mondial de Bruxelles in 1999.

☛ **780 Glasnevin Road, Amberley (State Highway 1, five minutes north of Amberley)**

Phone/fax: (03) 314 6900

Email: canterburyhouse@ibm.net

Website: www.canterburyhouse.com

Hours: for tasting and buying wines, same as restaurant.

Eating/other facilities: restaurant open daily 10am-5pm, evening dining and functions by arrangement.

Owner: Dr Michael Reid

Winemaker: Mark Rattray

Wines produced

○ Canterbury House Chardonnay, $18-20
Canterbury House Méthode Traditionelle, $23-25
Canterbury House Pinot Gris, $17-19
Canterbury House Riesling, $14-16
Canterbury House Sauvignon Blanc, $16-18

● Canterbury House Merlot, $21-23
Canterbury House Pinot Noir, $19-22

Chancellor Wines of Waipara

Helen and Tony Willy's interest in the wine business goes back to 1982 when they planted some sauvignon blanc and cabernet sauvignon vines in the Waipara Valley. They saw the similarities with Marlborough in climate and soil types, and figured there might be an extra bonus in the chalk and lime in these free-draining, stony soils. They were content to sell their fruit to other wineries until 1995 when they produced a sauvignon blanc under their own label.. Their wines have acquired a solid reputation – all the wines produced from estate grapes have won awards.

In 1998 they forged an alliance with another company and embarked on a programme of expansion. In 1999 they built a winery and wine sales outlet. But Helen says they will hold to their philosophy of producing wines of the highest quality from estate-grown grapes: 'Given time and patience Waipara is capable of producing not merely very good wines, but great wines measured by international standards.'

☞ **133 Mt Cass Road, Waipara**

Phone: (03) 314 6843

Fax: (03) 314 6894

Email: chancellor_wines@xtra.co.nz

Hours: for tasting and buying wines, by appointment.

Eating/other facilities: none.

Owner: Chancellor Estates Ltd

Winemaker: Kym Rayner

Wines produced

○ Chancellor Nor'wester Marlborough Chardonnay, $13-15
Chancellor Mt Cass Riesling, $13-15
Chancellor Mt Cass Waipara Sauvignon, $15-17
Chancellor Nor'wester Marlborough Sauvignon Blanc, $13-15

● Chancellor Marlborough Cabernet Merlot, $18-20
Chancellor Mt Cass Road Waipara Cabernet Sauvignon, $20-22

HURUNUI HOTEL

State Highway 7, Hurunui
phone (03) 314 4207

The Hurunui Hotel was granted its first licence in 1860, making it one of the oldest hotels in the country. Travellers had to cross the Hurunui River on the main route between Canterbury and Nelson in the north of the South Island, and, of course, it was also a watering hole for the farmers of the district – a place to collect mail and hear the latest news. After a devastating flood in 1868, the hotel was relocated to its present site where the original building still stands. It's made of limestone blocks held together and lined on the inside with a mixture of clay, tussock and lime. A little piece of history that's worth stopping for.

NOR'WESTER CAFÉ AND BAR

95 Main Rd, Amberley
phone (03) 314 9411

In 1998 this establishment won a Best Café Award and in 1999 a New Zealand Beef and Lamb Award of Excellence – great success for an eatery that set out simply to provide excellent food and coffee for the locals of the North Canterbury town of Amberley. It's named after the Nor'wester – the notorious hot, dry wind of Canterbury that brings with it the most spectacular skyscapes with a classic arch of cloud. The café has established a terrific reputation, and it's a good idea to book if you've time to plan ahead. Open every day from 11am for lunch and dinner.

Daniel Schuster Wines

Daniel Schuster is a founding figure in the Canterbury/ Waipara wine scene. He was winemaker at St Helena, the first commercial winery in Canterbury, and it was his pinot noir that stunned New Zealand in 1983 by taking a gold medal at the National Wine Competition. This was from Canterbury where, according to the view generally held in the early 1980s and before, you could not make good wines! Daniel Schuster Wines aims to produce a range of classically structured wines, both red and white. They have two vineyards, one on the limestone-rich soils of Omihi Hills planted in pinot noir. The other – the Petrie Vineyard – is on the gravelly plains near the Rakaia River and is planted in chardonnay and pinot noir. The winery is open for tastings, and tours can be arranged. There's a barbecue area by the landscaped lake and visitors are welcome to bring a picnic and 'cook their own'.

☞ **192 Reeces Road, Amberley**

Phone: (03) 314 5901

Fax: (03) 314 5902

Email: dswines@ihug.co.nz

Hours: wine tasting and buying seven days 10am-5pm.

Eating/other facilities: barbecue area, winery tours by appointment.

Owners: The Schuster, McCauley and Petrie families

Winemaker: Daniel Schuster

Wines produced

○ Daniel Schuster Canterbury Chardonnay, $19-22
Daniel Schuster Petrie Vineyard Selection
  Chardonnay, $25-28

● Daniel Schuster Pinot Noir, $19-22
Daniel Schuster Omihi Hills Selection Pinot Noir,
  $30-34

Fiddler's Green Wines _____

To win a silver medal for your first vintage is pretty good going. Fiddler's Green released their first riesling in 1997 and won silver at that year's Liquorland Top 100 International Wine Competition. The next year they produced their first sauvignon blanc and another award-winning riesling. These are the only two varieties the vineyard is producing at the time of writing, but they hope to release their pinot noir in 2001, and a chardonnay and méthode traditionelle in the following years. Fiddler's Green is owned by Christchurch lawyer Barry Johns and his wife Jennie. Their son Ben manages the vineyard. Barry has always had a passion for wine. He decided to learn about grapegrowing with wine writer Don Beaven and that led to the decision for him and Jennie to begin their own commercial venture. High quality, estate-grown wines are their aim and they're certainly off to a good start.

☛ **246 Georges Road, Waipara**

Phone: (03) 314 6979

Fax: (03) 314 6978

Email: fiddler@xtra.co.nz

Hours: Monday-Saturday 11am-5pm, October to May.

Eating/other facilities: none.

Owners: Barry and Jennie Johns

Winemaker: Petter Evans

Wines produced
○ Fiddler's Green Riesling, $15-17
  Fiddler's Green Sauvignon Blanc, $16-18

DYLANS COUNTRY COTTAGES

Postmans Road, RD1, Kaikoura
phone (03) 319 5473
fax (03) 319 5425
email: dylans.cs@clear.net.nz

$$

Tucked away at the base of the rugged seaward Kaikoura mountain range is a working lavender farm with two self-contained cottages offering a B&B facility. Both cottages are clad in rough-sawn timber, finished in macrocarpa, which was felled and milled on the property, and are very private. The breakfast menu features organically home-grown produce.

GRASMERE LODGE

phone (03) 318 8407
fax (03) 318 8263
email: retreat@grasmere.
co.nz
website: http://grasmere.
co.nz

$$$

This is super luxury! In 1998
the United States publication
*Andrew Harper's Hideaways
of the Year* picked Grasmere
Lodge as one of the world's
best. It's near Arthur's Pass
National Park; a high country
station set among 7000-foot
peaks, and just 90 minutes'
drive from Christchurch. An
historic homestead from the
days of the early European
settlers in Canterbury, it's
been refurbished as a very
stylish lodge. The
Craigieburn Range in the
Southern Alps provides a
stunning backdrop. Grasmere
Lodge comes complete with
an award-winning chef and an
impressive cellar of New
Zealand wines, with some
companion bottles from
France and Australia.

Floating Mountain

Winemaker Mark Rattray and his wife Michelle
established their Mark Rattray Vineyard in 1993 after
seven years' involvement with Waipara Springs Vineyard.
The property lies in the foothills of Mt Grey, the Maori
name for which is Maukatere and the English translation
'floating mountain'. When Mark was appointed
winemaker for Canterbury House he decided that from his
own property he would concentrate on producing less
wine but of the highest quality. It seemed a good time to
make a name change from Mark Rattray Vineyard as well.
Floating Mountain wines might take a bit of finding but it
will be worth the hunt.

☛ **418 Omihi Road, Waipara**
Phone/fax: (03) 314 6710
Email: markrattray@xtra.co.nz
Hours: by appointment.
Eating/other facilities: none.
Owners: Mark and Michelle Rattray
Winemaker: Mark Rattray

Wines produced
○ Floating Mountain Chardonnay, $35-38

● Floating Mountain Pinot Noir, $35-39

Glenmark Wines

Glenmark was the first winery to open in Waipara and
owner John McCaskey must be credited with having the
vision to see the winemaking potential of the area. What's
more, he saw it much earlier than most. But he had to
have tenacity – the first vines he planted in 1965 were all
lost after heavy flooding. This was particularly ironic,

given that one of the major difficulties facing growers is to ensure the supply of water during the dry summer months. The Glenmark Irrigation Scheme solved that problem, and in 1981 John re-established his vineyard, still convinced that Waipara was a good grapegrowing area. In 1986 his winery was completed.

Glenmark sheep station has been in the McCaskey family for over 50 years. It's sited in the lee of the Weka Pass and is surrounded by limestone hills. Glenmark doesn't produce a large quantity of wine but it has certainly produced some medal winners. The Waipara Red – a cabernet sauvignon-based wine – has won many awards, and the chardonnay and dry riesling have both won golds.

☛ **MacKenzies Road, Waipara**

Phone/fax: (03) 314 6828

Email: highclere@xtra.co.nz

Hours: for tasting and buying wines, open 11am-5pm seven days during school holidays, otherwise by appointment.

Eating/other facilities: café, offering simple but excellent food, is open 11am-5pm, Fridays-Sundays, October to April.

Owner: John McCaskey

Winemakers: Kym Rayner and John McCaskey

Wines produced

○ Glenmark Triple Peaks (dry and medium), $11-13
Glenmark Weka Plains Chardonnay, $22-24
Glenmark Weka Plains Gewürztraminer $22-24
Glenmark Weka Plains Riesling (dry and medium), $17-20
Glenmark Weka Plains Sauvignon Blanc (available through the winery only), $25-27
Glenmark Waipara White, $12-14

MOUNTFORD VINEYARD LODGE

434 Omihi Road, Waipara, North Canterbury
phone (03) 314 6819
fax (03) 314 6820

$$$

This was voted by *North & South* magazine as one of the three best new luxury lodges in New Zealand in 1999. The accommodation is colonial in style, and has every modern comfort. The extra bonus is an awe-inspiring view across the vineyard to the Southern Alps.

THE OLD GLENMARK VICARAGE

161 Church Road, Waipara
phone/fax (03) 314 6775
website: www.friars.co.nz/
hosts/glenmark.html

$$$

Glenmark Station was one of the early runholdings developed by European settler families in North Canterbury. The church and vicarage came later in 1906, and the latter has been beautifully restored and modernised for guests' comfort. Breakfast is traditional farmhouse fare, served in the farmhouse kitchen. These days views from the lovely old kauri building are of rolling hills covered with vines, rather than dotted with sheep as in a previous era.

● Glenmark Weka Plains Pinot Noir, $20-22
Glenmark Waipara Red, $15-27
Glenmark Vicarage Port, $22-24

Mountford Vineyard _____

A luxury homestay at a vineyard – it doesn't come much better than that. The Eatons planted the vineyard in 1991 and released their first wines in 1998. They grow only chardonnay and pinot noir.

Michael and Buffy Eaton's home is a marriage of something very Kiwi and something very French provincial. It has an exterior cladding of corrugated iron and sits facing a symmetrical terrace and vineyards stretching towards the Southern Alps. And it works wonderfully – the January 1999 issue of *North & South* magazine voted Mountford one of the three best new luxury lodges in New Zealand. The interior of the house is just as lovely, enhanced by Michael's paintings – he's been a professional artist for longer than he's been a vineyard owner. If you can get together a minimum of 10 people, you can book the lodge for special events. And Buffy is a superb cook!

☞ **434 Omihi Road, Waipara**

Phone: (03) 314 6819

Fax: (03) 314 6820

Hours: for tasting and buying wines, by appointment.

Eating/other facilities: luxury lodge accommodation.

Owners: Buffy and Michael Eaton

Winemaker: C P Lin (Chuny Pin)

Wines produced

○ Mountford Chardonnay, $30-33

● Mountford Pinot Noir, $30-34

Pegasus Bay

Surrounded by the rolling hills of the Cheviot Dale Range and set amongst landscaped gardens, this winery is truly a family affair. In 1986 the vineyard was established by Ivan Donaldson, his wife Chris, and their four sons. Ivan is a Christchurch medical specialist and wine columnist, and he and Chris remain very involved in their wine business. Having trained in Australia, their son Matthew has joined them as a winemaker. His brother Edward, who trained as a chef, runs the vineyard restaurant and is the marketing manager for Pegasus Bay.

The winery is a delight to visit – the wines are of high quality, the setting is gorgeous – be sure to walk through the gardens down to the lake – and the food is out of this world. When time permits, classical concerts are held in the natural outdoor amphitheatre (the hills protect you from the cold nip of the easterly winds). In recent years soprano Dame Malvina Major has featured as well as the Christchurch Symphony Orchestra. The family love of music is also reflected in the names of their reserve wines.

☞ **Stockgrove Road, Waipara**

Phone/fax: (03) 314 6869

Email: pegasus.bay.winery@xtra.co.nz

Hours: for tasting and buying wines, daily 10.30am-5pm.

Eating/other facilities: restaurant open 12 noon to 4pm daily.

Owners: Ivan and Chris Donaldson

Winemakers: Matthew Donaldson and Lynette Hudson

Wines produced

○ Pegasus Bay Aria (reserve late-picked riesling), $22-25
Pegasus Bay Chardonnay, $29-32

WAITUNA

McRaes Road, Waikari, North Canterbury
phone/fax (03) 314 4575

$-$$

About halfway between Christchurch and Hanmer Springs is this lovely, large historic homestead on 360 hectares of sheep and cattle farm. The building is listed with the Historic Places Trust, the oldest part dating from 1879. It's a great place for a farmstay.

WHITE MORPH MOTOR INN & RESTAURANT

92-94 The Esplanade, Kaikoura
phone (03) 319 5014
fax (03) 319 5015
email: morph@xtra.co.nz

$$-$$$

The White Morph is close to the centre of Kaikoura. It has great views of the Pacific Ocean and the restaurant is right on the waterfront. It's licensed and has a varied menu but, not surprisingly, it specialises in fresh fish and crayfish.

WINERY COTTAGE

State Highway, Amberley (just after the turn-off to the West Coast)

phone/fax (03) 314 6909

$$

This B&B cottage is close to Torlesse Winery in Waipara. It has generously sized bedrooms and modern ensuite bathrooms. An ideal spot to base yourself if you're contemplating some serious winery touring – especially if you like the idea of being collected and taken around on a horse-drawn wagon. This can be arranged, along with evening meals at the cottage.

Main Divide Chardonnay, $17-19

Pegasus Bay Finale (barrel fermented noble chardonnay) 375ml, $33-37

Pegasus Bay Riesling, $20-22

Main Divide Riesling, $13-15

Main Divide Sauvignon Blanc, $15-17

Pegasus Bay Sauvignon/Sémillon, $21-23

● Pegasus Bay Cabernet Merlot, $25-28

Pegasus Bay Maestro (reserve cabernet/merlot), $39-42

Main Divide Merlot Cabernet, $15-17

Pegasus Bay Pinot Noir, $35-38

Main Divide Pinot Noir, $17-20

Pegasus Bay Prima Donna (reserve pinot noir), $40-45

Torlesse Wines

Kym Rayner is a winemaker who comes from a grape-growing family in McLaren Vale in South Australia. He studied at the prestigious Roseworthy College and eventually brought his skills to New Zealand. Kym worked in Gisborne and Marlborough before coming to Canterbury. Torlesse was first established in the West Melton area in 1991, but in 1992 moved to Waipara. The winery, and Kym's skills, are shared with Glenmark. There is a strong focus on making Waipara wines, but Torlesse also makes other lines from grapes grown in selected vineyards in Marlborough and Canterbury.

☞ **Leff Lagen Drive, Waipara**

Phone/fax: (03) 377 1595 (sales), (03) 314 6929 (winery)

Email: aingertomlin@xtra.co.nz

Hours: for tasting and buying wines, seven days 11am-5pm.

Eating/other facilities: visitors are welcome to bring a picnic and enjoy it at the tables outside the winery's cellar door.

Owners: The Rayner, Tomlin, Blowers, Pharis and Fabris families

Winemaker: Kym Rayner

Wines produced

○ Torlesse Waipara Reserve Chardonnay, $25-27
Torlesse Unwooded Chardonnay, $13-15
Torlesse Canterbury Gewürztraminer, $14-16
Torlesse Marlborough Gewürztraminer, $16-18
Torlesse Riesling, $13-14
Torlesse Sauvignon Blanc, $16-18

● Torlesse Marlborough Cabernet Sauvignon, $13-15
Torlesse Waipara Reserve Cabernet Sauvignon
Merlot, $27-29
Torlesse Pinot Noir, $19-22
Torlesse Reserve Tawny Port, $20-22

Waipara Downs Wines _____

This 4.2-hectare vineyard is situated on a commercially producing 333-hectare prime sheep farm owned by Ruth and Keith Berry. Both were school teachers and Ruth still does a bit of relief teaching. Waipara Downs has been a farm since the 1930s, and when Ruth and Keith took it over it already had some land planted in vines. Keith has got farming in his blood and is happy to keep on with the sheep and help out with the vineyard. Ruth decided to take on the vineyard and threw herself into learning about viticulture and marketing. But it's a rough division of labour and both are happy with their decision to make a change from teaching. It's already given rise to a new family tradition – each year, around April/May, they have

MARINE ADVENTURES

Aquatic adventure is to be had from Kaikoura, the seaside settlement half way between Christchurch and Picton on the rugged east coast of the South Island. You can swim with the dolphins or seals, or go whale watching. The scenery is remarkable, with the mountains snow-clad for many months of the year, yet so close to the rugged coastline and sea. A number of companies cater for these unusual and fascinating marine adventures. The Visitor Information Centre has details.

DUST 'N' DIRT MOUNTAIN BIKING

phone/fax (03) 315 7233

The Hanmer Forest Park has great trails for mountain biking. There are some real challenges, but you can also take some quite gentle routes through a wide variety of both indigenous and exotic trees and enjoy the spectacular views.

HANMER SPRINGS

This alpine village is often covered in snow during winter, creating a dramatic backdrop for the region's activities. And one of its big attractions are the open-air thermal hot pools – ideal for when you want to just lie back and relax. There's quite a magic in being embraced by hot water with snow all around! A wide range of other activities can be enjoyed in the Hanmer district, from skiing in winter, mountain biking (a lot of competitive events are held here) and whitewater rafting, to forest walks and golf. Contact the Visitor Information Centre for details.

ALPINE HORSE SAFARIS

phone (03) 314 4293

If you want to 'earn' your wine experience, how about doing some trekking through the North Canterbury High Country? Alpine Horse Safaris offer treks taking from just a few hours to several days through interesting countryside.

a 'family pick'. Very much in the European tradition, about 60 members of the extended family gather to hand-pick a selection of vines. When the job's done they enjoy some of the previous year's vintage as a reward for the day's labour.

☛ **Bains Road (State Highway 7) Amberley**
Phone/fax: (03) 314 6873
Hours: for tasting and buying wines, by appointment only.
Eating/other facilities: none.
Owners: Ruth and Keith Berry
Winemaker: Phillippe Seguin

Wines produced

○ Waipara Downs Chardonnay, $19-21

● Waipara Downs Cabernet Sauvignon, $19-21
Waipara Downs Pinot Noir, $19-21
Waipara River Ruby Port, $15-17

Waipara Springs Wines _____

The group, which then included winemaker Mark Rattray, that planted the first vines at Waipara Springs in the early 1980s were among the trail-blazers of the district. They produced their first vintage in 1989 and were also among the first to see the potential of establishing a vineyard restaurant. An old woolshed and stables were converted and to this day it's a very popular place for a lingering weekend lunch. The food includes much of the excellent local produce for which the region is well known.

☛ **State Highway 1 (4km north of the Waipara**
bridge)
Phone/fax: (03) 314 6777

Email: shenderson@xtra.co.nz

Hours: for tasting and buying wines, 11am-5pm seven days except 24-26 December and 1 January.

Eating/other facilities: café open 11am-5pm same dates as winery, except closed 8 June-17 July.

Owners: The Grant and Moore families

Winemaker: Kim Rayner

Assistant Winemaker: Stephanie Grant

Wines produced

○ Waipara Springs Barrique Chardonnay, $21-23
Waipara Springs Lightly Oaked Chardonnay, $16-18
Waipara Springs Riesling, $16-18
Waipara Springs Sauvignon Blanc, $16-18

● Waipara Springs Cabernet Sauvignon, $18-20
Waipara Springs Pinot Noir, $28-31

Waipara West _____

There are strong family links in this venture, too. Paul Tutton and his artist wife, Olga Sienko, are the London-based branch and Vic Tutton, with her husband Lindsay Hill, live on the vineyard in Waipara, which was established in 1989. The winery was set up in 1997. The area is very picturesque and their wines are getting excellent notices. Paul Tutton is a wine merchant, and most of the vineyard's production is exported. However, as Vic says, 'Our aim is to grow premium fruit and make premium wines.' The 1998 pinot noir won gold at the Liquorland Wine Competition. Not surprisingly it's sold out, but the 1999 vintage is 'looking exciting'. Waipara West price their wines on the quality of the vintage. Pick up the phone and make an appointment to taste – it's worth the trip.

WEKA PASS RAILWAY

phone (03) 314 6813
or (03) 389 4078

Take a nostalgic ride through the wonderful limestone rock formations of the Weka Pass. The most beloved of these is Frog Rock, which seems to keep a close eye on who's going by on the road. This journey is possible because of the devotion of volunteer train buffs who, in 1983, decided to buy and restore this section of a former branch line. They have also restored a collection of veteran steam and diesel engines and carriages. The journey takes an hour-and-a-half (return). The trains leave at 11.30am and 2pm on the 1st and 3rd Sunday of each month, and also on public holidays.

COLMONELL WINE TRAILS AND WAGON TREKS

phone/fax (03) 314 6805

Everybody loves a Clydesdale. Imagine having a team of them drawing your wagon along the wine trail. With Colmonell Wine Trails and Wagon Treks you can do your wine tasting and vineyard lunching this way.

THE MAORI LEAP CAVE

phone/fax (03) 319 5023

Delve into the past with a visit to this sea cave, estimated to be over two million years old. Some of the stalactites and stalagmites themselves are thought to be 3000 years old. Tours take 40 minutes and there are six each day, departing from the Caves Restaurant on State Highway 1, not far from Kaikoura itself.

SURFING OR LOLLING ABOUT ON THE BEACH

As you travel north up State Highway 1, about half way between Waipara and Kaikoura is the little township of Cheviot. Take an eight kilometre detour to the beach at Gore Bay. There's excellent surfing to be had, a safe beach for swimmers, and the magnificent sight of tall fluted cliffs known as 'The Cathedrals'.

☛ **376 Ram Paddock Road, Amberley**

Phone: (03) 314 8330

Fax: (03) 314 8692

Hours: for buying wines, Monday to Friday 10am-4pm

Eating/other facilities: none.

Owners: Paul Tutton and Olga Sienko-Tutton, Lindsay Hill and Vic Tutton

Winemaker: Petter Evans

Wines produced

○ Waipara West Chardonnay, $21-26
Waipara West Riesling, $20-22
Waipara West Sauvignon Blanc, $18-20

● Waipara West Pinot Noir, $35-38
Waipara West Ram Paddock Red (cabernet sauvignon cabernet franc merlot), $19-21

canterbury

A grand total of 80 vineyards and 35 wineries is pretty impressive for a region that only two decades ago was said to be unsuitable for growing grapes! Canterbury has since produced some great pinot noir and chardonnay, along with excellent riesling, pinot gris, gewürztraminer and sauvignon blanc.

In the early 1970s Dr David Jackson of Lincoln University (then Lincoln College) began grape trials to establish the most suitable varieties for the region. In 1976, at a wine lecture held at Lincoln, a number of speakers from Auckland claimed that good wines couldn't be made in the South Island. Given the traditional rivalry between the two main islands of New Zealand, this was challenging stuff. It was also the spur for a number of people to get seriously involved in winemaking. Whatever the basis for that original claim, it has certainly been proved wrong.

From a viticultural point of view New Zealand has a cool climate. Of course, the further south, the cooler it gets. Canterbury also has a relatively low rainfall and is particularly suited to riesling, chardonnay and pinot noir. Long, dry autumns with warm days and cool nights let the grapes ripen slowly, producing high levels of acidity and extract.

Many of the wineries sell their product directly to the public, and Canterbury is a fabulous district for those who enjoy a vineyard lunch! An increasing number of wineries have opened a café or restaurant facility, and most are within reach of the central city in under an hour. It's possible to sample anything from a simple vineyard platter to the best of New Zealand cuisine.

Canterbury lamb has had an excellent reputation for many years, but the region produces a wide variety of delectable fare for locals and visitors to enjoy. Options for

REGIONAL HIGHLIGHTS

CANTERBURY FOOD AND WINE FESTIVAL

A showcase for the local wine and food industry, this annual festival is held in Hagley Park in the city in mid-February.

Contact Arch Stiller phone (03) 358 2252.

WORLD BUSKERS FESTIVAL

Towards the end of January each year, 10 days of international street theatre make the streets of Christchurch a very enjoyable if somewhat unpredictable place – you never know what acts you might come across.

Contact the Christchurch Arts Centre office phone (03) 363 2836.

FESTIVAL OF ROMANCE

From 5-14 February Christchurch dons rose-tinted spectacles and celebrates romance through music, theatre, dance and more.

Contact the Christchurch Arts Centre office phone (03) 363 2836.

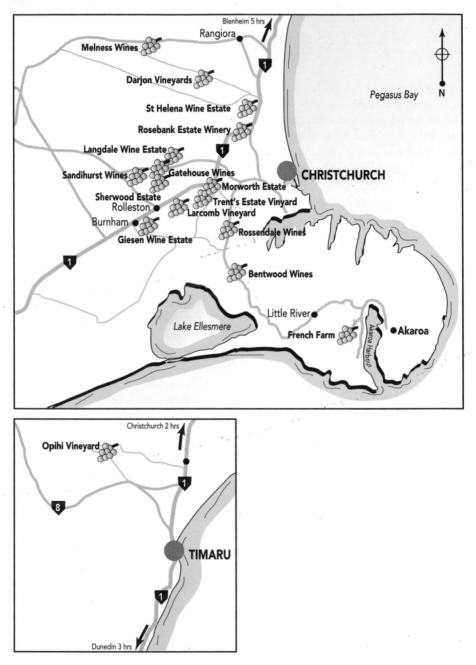

Blenheim 5 hrs
Rangiora
Melness Wines
Darjon Vineyards
St Helena Wine Estate
Rosebank Estate Winery
Langdale Wine Estate
Sandihurst Wines
Gatehouse Wines
Morworth Estate
Sherwood Estate
Rolleston
Trent's Estate Vinyard
Larcomb Vineyard
Burnham
Rossendale Wines
Giesen Wine Estate
Bentwood Wines
CHRISTCHURCH
Pegasus Bay
N
Little River
Lake Ellesmere
French Farm
Akaroa
Akaroa Harbour

Christchurch 2 hrs
Opihi Vineyard
TIMARU
Dunedin 3 hrs

accommodation are satisfyingly varied, too – historic homestays, cosy bed and breakfasts, luxurious lodges or modern hotels.

In February of each year the Canterbury Food and Wine Festival is held in Hagley Park, right in the centre of Christchurch. Generally at that time of the year the weather is warm and settled, and it is a marvellous opportunity to sip and sample your way through some crisp rieslings, spicy gewürztraminers, a plummy and velvety pinot noir or a lighter one with tamarillo overtones, or perhaps a lively and fruity chardonnay. The good thing, however, is that all these pleasures can be had the year round!

AUTHOR'S FAVOURITES

Giesen Botrytised Riesling

Opihi Pinot Gris

St Helena Pinot Noir

Sandihurst Pinot Noir

Sherwood Sauvignon Blanc

i Christchurch
Cnr Worcester Boulevard and Oxford Terrace
PO Box 2600
phone (03) 379 9629
fax (03) 377 2424
email: info@christchurchtourism.co.nz

Arthur's Pass
State Highway 73, Main Road
PO Box 8, Arthur's Pass 8190
phone (03) 318 9211
fax (03) 318 9271

Ashburton
Cnr East and Burnett Streets
phone/fax (03) 308 1064

Methven
Main Road
phone/fax (03) 302 8955

Mt Cook National Park
Bowen Drive
PO Box 5, Mt. Cook 8770
phone (03) 435 1186
fax (03) 435 1080

REGIONAL HIGHLIGHTS

BOOKS AND BEYOND

This annual Christchurch Book Festival is held at the beginning of June.

For further information contact the Events Team at the Christchurch City Council phone (03) 379 1660.

SHOWTIME CANTERBURY

A fortnight-long celebration that takes place around Canterbury's anniversary day on 12 November. It includes the annual A&P Show, the DB Draught New Zealand Trotting Cup Carnival and the Canterbury Draught New Zealand Cup.

For further information contact the Events Team at the Christchurch City Council phone (03) 379 1660.

the wineries

Bentwood Wines ————————

In 1990 Ray and Robyn Watson sold their Christchurch business and went to France with their two children. They were going to take a year 'to sit under a vine'. In fact they worked in a small vineyard in Entre de Mer, south of Bordeaux. Robyn says the French Algerians of the area 'couldn't do enough for us'. It was obviously a great experience.

On their return in 1991 they bought some land on Banks Peninsula. The next year they planted a vineyard with pinot blanc, pinot noir, riesling and gewürztraminer. 'Really, we established the vineyard as an interest to take us through to old age.' But it was an interest with a steep learning curve. It was time to consult with Dr David Jackson at Lincoln University, and Ray and Robyn count themselves fortunate to have also met Grant Whelan, one of the first winemakers at Lincoln.

Their first harvest was in 1995. Bentwood is a small, family vineyard, and the Watsons want to keep it that way so they don't have to employ a large regular staff. For that reason, although visitors are very welcome, they are asked to telephone to make a time for their visit.

Canterbury is fast gaining a reputation as a food lover's favourite destination. Apart from the delights of visiting the local wineries to sip the region's excellent pinot noirs, chardonnays and rieslings, visitors can sample the local salmon and lamb accompanied by mouth-watering fresh produce and followed by locally made cheeses, fresh berry fruits and hand-made chocolates. There is no shortage of excellent places to dine in Canterbury, and many of these can be found on the region's vineyards. The following selection offers a variety of areas, styles and cuisine.

☛ **Akaroa Highway, Tai Tapu, Canterbury**

Phone: (03) 329 6191

Fax: (03) 329 6192

Email: rrwatson@xtra.co.nz

Hours: tasting and purchasing by appointment only.

Eating/other facilities: none.

Owners: Ray and Robyn Watson

Winemaker: Grant Whelan

Wines produced

○ Bentwood Gewürztraminer, $14-16
  Bentwood Pinot Blanc, $16-18
  Bentwood Riesling, $13-15

● Bentwood Pinot Noir, $18-20

Darjon Vineyards

John Baker is in pursuit of his own Holy Grail, which is 'to make a pinot noir as good as that made by Danny Schuster in 1982 at St Helena'. At a time when John's involvement with winemaking was still just a hobby, he had given noted Canterbury winemaker Daniel Schuster a helping hand. 'I can still taste that wine,' says John. It turned out to be the first Canterbury wine to win a gold medal.

The hobby became a job when John and his wife Michelle established Darjon Vineyards in 1989. Their own vineyard produces a Darjon Home Block pinot noir and riesling. Marlborough growers supply them with fruit for a sémillon/sauvignon blanc and a blush wine.

As well as selling their own wines, Darjon acts as agent for a wide range of other New Zealand and Australian boutique wineries. They have also established a delightful vineyard restaurant. Many of the wines on their list are available by the glass and the place has the convivial atmosphere of a country wine bar.

ANNIE'S WINE BAR AND RESTAURANT

South Quad of the Christchurch Arts Centre (opens up off Worcester Boulevard)
phone (03) 365 0566

Annie's specialises in gourmet local cuisine with a Pacific flavour. The bar has a great wine list featuring the finest wines of Canterbury and an interesting selection of boutique wines from around New Zealand. Open seven days 11am until late.

BARCELONA

Cnr Oxford Terrace and Worcester Boulevard
phone (03) 377 2100

This is a city wine bar with a relaxed atmosphere and totally delectable food. It's also refreshing to find a café that offers flexibility in terms of meal size. Open seven days 12 noon-3pm for lunch and 6pm-10pm for dinner.

BOLOGNA

6 Papanui Road, Christchurch
phone (03) 379 7497

A tiny BYO restaurant serving traditional Italian food and specialising in the most delicious pizzas. You can also order to take away. Open seven days from 6pm.

LE BON BOLLI

Cnr Worcester Boulevard &
Montreal Street, Christchurch
phone (03) 374 9444

This award-winning restaurant offers a wonderful combination of delicatessen, bar, restaurant and brasserie dining both indoors and on the 'Parisienne Pavement'. It's situated in the area that has become known as the 'cultural precinct'. Fully licensed. Open seven days, 10am until late.

☞ **North Eyre Road, Swannanoa, North Canterbury**

Phone: (03) 312 6045

Fax: (03) 312 6544

Hours: for tasting and buying wines, as per restaurant. Please phone prior to visiting.

Eating/other facilities: restaurant open noon-5pm on Saturday and Sunday and most public holidays. Candlelit dining Saturdays from 7pm. Bookings essential.

Owners: Michelle and John Baker

Winemaker: John Baker

Wines produced:

○ Darjon Homeblock Riesling, $16-18
Darjon Marlborough Sauvignon Blanc/Sémillon, $16-18

● Darjon Homeblock Pinot Noir, $22-24

Wines are also produced using Marlborough fruit in some seasons.

French Farm _____

It was touch and go as to whether France or England would be the first European country to colonise New Zealand in the nineteenth century. A French whaler, Captain Jean Langlois, paid local Ngai Tahu 6000 francs for 12,500 hectares of Banks Peninsula in 1838. Travel by sailing ship took weeks, of course, and by the time he arrived back from France with a group of 63 settlers the British had raised their flag.

Nevertheless there is still quite a French flavour to the township of Akaroa and a number of settlements around the harbour. The French Farm winery nestles into one of the valleys on the opposite side of the harbour to Akaroa itself. With stunning views, it was built to reflect the area's

Canterbury House Winery, Waipara

The Donaldson Family, Pegasus Bay, Waipara

Chancellor Wines, Waipara

Fiddler's Green, Waipara

Hot air ballooning, Canterbury

Opihi Vineyard, Canterbury

Historic Antigua Boat Sheds, Canterbury

DAVID WALL

Langdale Wine Estate, Canterbury

French heritage. It has arched windows with wooden shutters, and roofing tiles imported from Marseilles. There is an à la carte restaurant and an outdoor barbecue facility.

Banks Peninsula has a microclimate suitable for growing chardonnay and pinot noir. The vineyards were established on a north-facing loam clay slope in 1989 and their first vintage was in 1993.

☛ **French Farm Valley Road, No 2 RD, Akaroa**

Phone: (03) 304 5784

Fax: (03) 304 5785

Email: siparker@frenchfarm.co.nz

Hours: for tasting and buying wines, as per restaurant.

Eating/other facilities: à la carte restaurant open 10am-5pm seven days.

Owner: James Ullrich

Winemaker: Mark Leonard

Wines produced

○ French Farm Chardonnay, $22-24

● French Farm Pinot Noir, $24-27

Gatehouse Wines _____

The stony soils of the Waimakariri flood plain are home to the vineyards of Gatehouse Wines. Pete Gatehouse was experimenting with making fruit wines back in the 1960s. He had some successes and caught the winemaking bug. He began planting his vines in the early 1980s, his winery was established in 1989 and he is now totally involved with the industry. He is winemaker for a number of vineyards, lectures in wine science at Lincoln University and works as a consultant to a number of other wineries in the South Island.

C'EST LA VIE

33 Rue Lavaud, Akaroa, Banks Peninsula
phone (03) 304 7314

Caters for food lovers, providing fine French cuisine with seafood specialities. BYO licence. Open seven days, 6pm until late. Bookings essential.

MISCEO CAFÉ & BAR

Cnr Ilam and Clyde Roads, Fendalton, Christchurch
phone (03) 351 8011

This café, bar and restaurant offers indoor and outdoor dining. It's very popular, has some intriguing copper features in its décor, provides good food with excellent service, and is fun to go to. Fully licensed. Open seven days 10am until late.

PEDRO'S

143 Worcester Street,
Christchurch
phone (03) 379 7668

This award-winning restaurant is also one of Christchurch's most enduring. It's one of the few Spanish restaurants in New Zealand, and specialises in seafood and lamb. It has a well-deserved reputation for using only the freshest of produce. BYO licence. Open Tuesday-Saturday from 6pm until late.

STRONECHRUBIE

Scenic Highway 72, Mt
Somers, Mid-Canterbury
phone (03) 303 9814

Chef Robert Koller and his wife Christine opened Stronechrubie in 1992, specialising in 'New Zealand produce, the European way'. It has a BYO licence, serves breakfast and dinner, and the cuisine is truly outstanding.

☞ **Jowers Road, RD6, Christchurch**

Phone/fax: (03) 342 9682

Hours: for tasting and buying wines, 11am-5pm seven days. Peter will also organise winery tours.

Eating/other facilities: café open same hours as winery.

Owner: The Gatehouse family

Winemaker: Peter Gatehouse

Wines produced

○ Gatehouse Chardonnay, $14-16
Gatehouse Late Pick Chardonnay 375ml, $23-26
Gatehouse Riesling, $9-14

● Gatehouse Merlot, $21-23
Gatehouse Pinot Noir, $10-12

Giesen Wine Estate _____

The three Giesen brothers – Theo, Alex and Marcel – came from a family involved in quarrying and construction. But, as was common in Germany, the family also had a small plot of grapevines and made wine for themselves. They came to New Zealand looking for 'New World opportunity'. Originally they worked for a Canterbury construction company, but when they couldn't find the kind of wine they liked at home, especially dry riesling, it spurred them on to buy some land for planting. Riesling flourishes in a cool climate, so Canterbury was their choice.

The brothers now own the region's largest winery, with 45 hectares of vineyards in Canterbury and Marlborough, and they export widely. Over the years they've expanded their range of grape varieties, but they've earned classic wine status with their series of botrytised rieslings.

☞ **Burnham School Road, Burnham, Christchurch**

Phone: (03) 347 6729

Fax: (03) 347 6450

Email: info@giesen.co.nz

Hours: 10am-5pm Monday to Saturday.

Eating/other facilities: none.

Owners: Theo, Alex and Marcel Giesen

Winemaker: Andrew Blake

Wines produced

○ Giesen Chardonnay, $16-18
Giesen Reserve Canterbury Chardonnay, $30-33
Giesen Reserve Marlborough Chardonnay, $21-23
Giesen Late Harvest, $22-24
Giesen Riesling, $11-12
Giesen Riesling Extra Dry, $15-17
Giesen Sauvignon Blanc, $14-16
Giesen Voyage Méthode Traditionelle, $21-24

● Giesen Pinot Noir, $22-25

Langdale Wine Estate _____

Lew Stribling, the business manager of the group involved with Langdale Wine Estate, says that he's always loved the countryside and when he was growing up he often visited a farm. He says he wanted to do something on the land, 'but not in traditional mode. I wanted to retain control of the creative process.'

The estate has 4.5 hectares planted in pinot noir, chardonnay, riesling, pinot gris and breidecker. All the grapes are hand-picked, and most of their wines are made on site. You can hear his love of the business when Lew talks about the challenge of following the process from the vineyard to the final product. There are always so many variables. 'We're really competing with nature', he says.

THE CHARLOTTE JANE

110 Papanui Road, Merivale, Christchurch
phone (03) 355 1028
fax (03) 355 8882

$$–$$$

Bed and breakfast in sheer luxury can be had here in the suburb of Merivale, close to the city. A two-year restoration job was done on this historic Christchurch home, providing 10 spacious and beautifully decorated luxury bedrooms.

GUNYAH COUNTRY LODGE

Sleemans Road, Glenroy, Darfield
phone (03) 318 6800
fax (03) 318 6504
email: relax@gunyah.co.nz

$$$

This is one of Canterbury's oldest homesteads. Built in 1913 for the son of former Prime Minister Sir John Hall, it sits at the foot of the Southern Alps and offers spectacular views beyond its beautiful grounds. Ideally placed to take advantage of a range of activities including skiing, golf, croquet, jet-boating and bush walking.

HADLEIGH HOMESTAY

6 Eversleigh Street,
Christchurch
phone/fax (03) 355 7174

$$$

Another fine restoration job
has been done on this
historic Christchurch house.
The owners have a passion
for art and many of the works
in their collection are by New
Zealand artists. It's a bed and
breakfast facility, centrally
located.

KAWATEA FARMSTAY

Okains Bay, Banks Peninsula
phone/fax (03) 304 8621

$$-$$$

Designed by the noted
Canterbury architect Hurst
Seager and built in 1900, the
homestead of Kawatea – a
working farm of 1400 acres –
provides a very enjoyable
farmstay experience. Owners
Kerry and Judy are third
generation farmers, running
sheep and cattle over the hill
country property.

'It's not a question of winning, but finding a workable solution.'

☛ **Langdales Road, West Melton**

Phone: (03) 342 6266

Fax: (03) 342 4059

Hours: for tasting and buying wines, same hours as restaurant.

Eating/other facilities: Langdale Vineyard Restaurant is open Tuesday-Thursday 11am-4pm (summer to 5pm), Friday and Saturday 11am-late, Sunday and public holidays 11am-5pm (summer to 6pm).

Owners: Shareholders

Winemaker: Carl Bunn

Wines produced

○ Langdale Breidecker, $12-14
Langdale Barrel Fermented Chardonnay, $16-18
Langdale Pinot Gris, $16-18
Langdale Riesling, $16-18
Langdale Marlborough Sauvignon Blanc, $16-18

● Langdale Petit Syrah Reserve, $26-29
Langdale Pinot Noir, $18-20

Larcomb Vineyard _____

It was two veterinarians who gave Canterbury its first vineyard restaurant. John Thom and his wife Julie Wagner were convinced that the best way to sell wine was to have a place where people could taste the wine while eating good food and enjoying the company of friends. So the couple restored the old farm buildings on their property just south of Christchurch and established a delightful vineyard bar. They had planted their first vines in 1980 and in 1988 John gave up his vet practice and went into winemaking full time.

Larcomb vineyard is only 20 minutes from the centre of Christchurch and it didn't take long for it to become very popular with locals. Most of their wine was sold over the vineyard counter, which was the way John and Julie wanted it.

In 1995 Warren and Michelle Barnes bought the vineyard. They were very experienced in the hospitality and food business and initially thought that was where they would concentrate their efforts, leasing out the vineyard. But winemaking can be a seductive business! It was a good business decision but it also reflected their growing interest in wine production.

Adding to the space offered by the restored stables, they extended the seating and built an all-year-round facility, which continues to be a favourite venue for a relaxed vineyard lunch. They will, however, keep to their current wine production levels because they like being able to serve and sell their own wines, all of which are sold through the vineyard.

☞ **Cnr Main South Road (State Highway 1) and Larcombs Road, Weedons**

Phone: (03) 347 8909

Fax: (03) 347 8902

Hours: for tasting and buying wines, same as restaurant.

Eating/other facilities: restaurant with extensive indoor and outdoor seating open summer 11am-5pm Tuesday-Sunday, winter Friday-Sunday. And Larcomb's has become the home of the 'Rattle Rafters' Barn Dances and 'Murder in the Stables' with Court Jesters.

Owners: Warren and Michelle Barnes

Winemaker Consultant: Alan McCorkindale

THE OLD SHIPPING OFFICE

3 Church Street, Akaroa, Banks Peninsula
phone (03) 304 7559
fax (03) 304 7455
freephone 0800 4L HOTEL
$$$

A century ago this was the shipping office for Akaroa. In 1995 it was completely renovated and now offers two comfortable bedrooms. It's managed by the owners of the hotel next door, so guests can make use of room service facilities. Just steps away on the main street of Akaroa is a range of good restaurants.

ROCKVILLA GUEST INN

24 Marriner Street, Sumner,
Christchurch
phone (03) 326 6985
fax (03) 326 6845

$$

Only 20 minutes out of
Christchurch city, the seaside
village of Sumner has eagerly
embraced the idea of a café
society. It's also close to some
charming walks. Dating back
to the early twentieth century,
Rockvilla, as its name
suggests, is made out of local
rock and is architecturally
interesting. The guest rooms
are comfortable and have
private balconies.

STONEYBROOK

Okuti Valley Road, Little River,
Banks Peninsula
phone (03) 325 1208
fax (03) 325 1111

$$$

The native bush and birdlife
in the Okuti Valley are worth
a visit on their own – as you'll
discover when you turn off
the main highway (before
going up the hill to Akaroa).
Stoneybrook's self-contained
apartment has a distinctly

Wines produced

○ Larcomb Breidecker, $14-16
  Larcomb Chardonnay, $17-19
  Larcomb Pinot Gris, $16-18
  Larcomb Riesling, $16-18
  Larcomb Sauvignon Blanc, $16-18

● Larcomb Pinot Noir, $19-22

Melness Wines ───────────

In the 1860s David Paton McKay left the small coastal
village of Melness in the far north of Scotland, where he
was born, and sailed across the world to become one of
the early European settlers of Banks Peninsula. Melness
Wines is named in his memory – and New World
winemakers still have some of his pioneering spirit!

David McKay was the grandfather of Norma Marshall.
She and her husband, Colin, had become hobby winemakers in the early 1980s, using surplus grapes from
the Lincoln University vineyard. They took their hobby
seriously, attending seminars at Lincoln and touring the
best wineries and vineyards in France with Dr David
Jackson.

In 1987 they bought land at Cust, in North Canterbury. They planted their first vines in 1990 but, initially,
only to provide enough grapes to make wine for
themselves. They were then teachers at a local Christchurch high school, but teaching lost out when the hobby
took over and became a full-scale commercial venture.
They have no regrets about the move. Colin says this last
year has been the best year of his life.

Although not officially registered as organic, Melness
applies the principles of sustainable viticulture. Rasp-
berries, strawberries, apples and vegetables grow along-
side the vines, which are treated only with non-chemical
fertilisers and sprays. Melness Wines is a participant in the

Integrated Wine Production scheme (the IWP came into being in the mid 1990s and now has over 150 members in New Zealand and Switzerland – members are committed to taking a sustainable approach to viticultural management and use organic sprays whenever possible).

The Marshalls have trialled 11 grape varieties and have decided the three best suited to the area are pinot noir, chardonnay and gewürztraminer. They do make other wines but for these the fruit is sourced from other areas.

☞ **1816 Main Road, Cust, North Canterbury**

Phone: (03) 312 5402

Fax: (03) 312 5466

Hours: for tasting and buying wines, same hours as café.

Eating/other facilities: the on-site café is open 10.30am–5pm.

Owners: Colin and Norma Marshall

Winemakers: Matthew Donaldson and Lynette Hudson

Wines produced

○ Melness Chardonnay, $21-23
Melness Gewürztraminer, $15-17
Melness Riesling, $15-17
Melness Rosé, $8-9
Melness Sauvignon Blanc, $14-16

● Melness Cabernet Sauvignon, $16-19
Melness Cabernet Sauvignon/Merlot, $26-29
Melness Pinot Noir, $30-33

(cont'd)
French ambience that is entirely appropriate given the history of the area. The two large upstairs bedrooms look out over the Okuti River that runs through the property's well-maintained gardens.

STRONECHRUBIE

Scenic Highway 72, Mt Somers, Mid-Canterbury
phone/fax (03) 303 9814

$$

This is a country restaurant with accommodation attached – a wonderful concept common in Europe but not so easy to find in New Zealand. There are eight individual chalets set in a quiet garden with views to the Southern Alps, including the skifield of Mt Hutt.

TAKAMATUA B&B

Bell's Road, Takamatua, Banks Peninsula
phone (03) 304 7499

$$-$$$

David Thurston is one of Canterbury's finest furniture makers. Like many of the talented craftspeople in the

(cont'd)

region, he and his wife Sue have chosen to live on Banks Peninsula, where David utilised his talents by building the house and most of its furniture. There are three guest bedrooms, each featuring a stylish sleigh bed made from native wood. Shaded by old walnut trees, the property has a swimming pool and both croquet and petanque are on offer.

THE WORCESTER OF CHRISTCHURCH

15 Worcester Boulevard, Christchurch
phone (03) 365 0936
fax (03) 364 6299
freephone 0800 365015
email: the.worcester@clear.net.nz

$$$

In the heart of Christchurch's 'cultural precinct', this delightful character house offers three guest rooms. It's on the doorstep of the Arts Centre, the Museum, the Botanic Gardens and a wide choice of cafés and restaurants.

Morworth Estate

Until very recently Morworth Estate wines were made entirely from hand-harvested grapes from the owners' own vineyard. Sourcing fruit from other areas is something they've only just begun to do. But behind this decision is a commitment to quality. After six years in the business Leonie and Chris Morkane acknowledge that not all varieties are suited to their vineyard and they're now buying from Marlborough for the production of their sauvignon blanc and chardonnay. The grapes their 12 hectares do suit, however, are riesling, pinot noir, pinot gris and gewürztraminer.

It was a long-standing interest in grape and wine production that tempted Chris and Leonie to see what would succeed on their Broadfield property on the outskirts of Christchurch. This interest grew into a determination to produce quality varietal wines and the decision to build a 200 tonne capacity winery at Broadfield. Construction is now under way, and the winery should be open in the year 2000.

The winery will also be an art gallery and functions centre. The tasting room has been designed to accommodate full exhibitions and the Southern Alps will be the backdrop for open air concerts.

With their daughter Sarah, the viticulturist in the enterprise, Leonie and Chris are making some changes in their vineyard practices to produce wines with greater intensity, capitalising on the extended warm, dry autumns that give them the ability to delay harvest times. They say that reducing crop yields and having an open canopy management regime is starting to produce wines that show great promise.

☛ **Shands Road, Christchurch**
   Phone: (03) 349 5014
   Fax: (03) 349 4419
   Email: morworth@ihug.co.nz

Hours: 10am-4pm – winery tours by appointment.

Eating/other facilities: winery intended to double as an exhibitions centre and concert venue.

Owners: Chris and Leonie Morkane

Winemakers: Alan McCorkindale and Andrew Byers

Wines produced

○ Morworth Estate Breidecker, $12-14
  Morworth Estate Chardonnay, $20-22
  Morworth Estate Riesling, $15-17
  Morworth Estate Marlborough Sauvignon Blanc
    $18-20

● Morworth Estate Pinot Noir, $22-25

Opihi Vineyard _____

Although established in the early 1990s, the first commercial production from the South Canterbury Opihi Vineyard wasn't released until November 1996, and since then their wines have been available only in South Canterbury. They are definitely worth searching out, though – in 1998 their pinot gris took Gold in the Auckland Liquorland Easter Show and they are beginning to get orders from the North Island.

Opihi is the district 30 kilometres inland from the city of Timaru. This Maori name means 'the place of good growth'. Certainly the sheltered, north-facing slope chosen for the vineyard is ideal for the production of high quality grapes. The South Canterbury climate allows for long, slow ripening and the wines have intense fruit flavours.

Colin and Brenda have long been arable farmers. They had a spare paddock in front of their house and Brenda's brother, John Brough, who owns Sandihurst Wines at West Melton near Christchurch, kept saying, 'I'm sure your hill could grow grapes.' Colin and Brenda's first commercial production was made at Sandihurst.

THE CHRISTCHURCH ARTS CENTRE

Worcester Boulevard, between Rolleston Avenue and Montreal Street
phone (03) 363 2836

In the neo-Gothic buildings of the University of Canterbury's first home there is now a busy, thriving arts and crafts centre. It contains retail outlets for artists and studio spaces where the public can talk with artists and watch them at work. There are also galleries and art house cinemas. The Arts Centre is the home of Christchurch's professional theatre, The Court, and there's also a wide range of cafés. A craft market with a fascinating array of stalls is open during the weekend.

ROBERT McDOUGALL ART GALLERY AND THE CANTERBURY MUSEUM

The city's art gallery is adjacent to the Canterbury Museum and together they tell the story of the region's art and cultural history. Both the gallery and the museum open out onto the Botanic Gardens.

TAKE A RIDE ON A PUNT

Idle your way through the Botanic Gardens and the western stretches of the Avon River, which meanders through the city, and let somebody else do the hard work.

Book a punt ride at the Christchurch Visitor Information Centre, or through Punting In The Park, at the southern end of Rolleston Avenue next to Christchurch Hospital. phone (03) 366 0337

Brenda says they're looking to produce easy drinking wines in an off-dry to medium style. They have recently converted an old limestone cottage into a wine tasting venue and have created a relaxed atmosphere where vineyard platters are served and barbecue and picnic facilities are provided.

☞ **Goulds Road, Pleasant Point, South Canterbury**

Phone: (03) 614 7232

Fax: (03) 614 7234

Hours: tasting and buying wines by appointment. Please phone before visiting.

Eating/other facilities: winery platter provided for tasters. Picnic area and barbecue facilities available.

Owners: Colin and Brenda Lyon

Winemaker: Tony Coakley

Wines produced

○ Opihi Chardonnay, $18-20
Opihi Müller Thurgau, $10-11
Opihi Pinot Gris, $18-20
Opihi Riesling, $15-17

● Opihi Pinot Noir, $15-18

Rosebank Estate Winery ──────

Canterbury locals were quick to embrace the pleasures of wine and lunch. At Rosebank they extend the options even further – there's a cricket oval, a petanque court, swings and slides, and a large rose garden. To celebrate the development of the cricket oval they released a series of 1996 white wines called the Rosebank Cricket Collection. The label shows a game of cricket played at Halfpenny Down in 1777.

Rosebank Estate is the closest winery to Christchurch

and has the atmosphere of a country wine bar. They source their grapes from Canterbury and Marlborough.

☞ **Cnr Johns Road & Groynes Drive, Harewood, Christchurch**

Phone: (03) 323 8539

Fax: (03) 323 8538

Email: briansh@rosebank.co.nz

Hours: for tasting and buying wines, 10am-5pm.

Eating/other facilities: restaurant open seven days for lunch (closed Mondays and Tuesdays from May to October), phone: (03) 323 7353.

Accommodation: motels on site, phone: (03) 323 8224.

Owners: Brian and Margaret Shackel

Winemaker: Kym Rayner

Wines produced

○ Rosebank Marlborough Chardonnay, $15-17
Rosebank Canterbury Chardonnay, $15-17
Rosebank Marlborough Riesling, $12-14
Rosebank Marlborough Sauvignon Blanc, $15-17

● Rosebank Marlborough Merlot/Cabernet Franc, $14-16

THE BOTANIC GARDENS

Follow up that latte with a stroll round the superb Botanic Gardens, off Rolleston Avenue and at the end of the Worcester Boulevard (just over the road from the Arts Centre). The Canterbury Association, as the prime movers behind the European settlement of Christchurch, were responsible for the setting aside of 30 hectares of rich alluvial soil that were subsequently planted with introduced species and native plants. This broad and peaceful expanse in the centre of the city, with the Avon River running through it, is especially stunning in spring with its masses of daffodils and crocuses, and in autumn, when its many species of European trees display a rich palette of warm colours.

Rossendale Wines —————

In the 1980s Brent Rawstron was already a successful exporter of high quality beef. But times and farming practices were changing and he saw a need to diversify. He and his wife Shirley also saw the potential for establishing a vineyard.

What started as a pragmatic response has become a fascination. It's not often in the farming life-cycle that it's possible to do all parts of the process, and Brent and

WHITE WATER RAFTING AND KAYAKING

Rangitata Rafts, Peel Forest, RD20, South Canterbury phone 0800 251 251

If you're feeling energetic, the braided rivers of Canterbury offer various grades of thrill; there are gentle rapids for the novice and foaming white waters for the experienced daredevil.

WALKING IN NATIVE BUSH

The Banks Peninsula Track is a four-day walk that begins and ends in Akaroa. There are lush stands of bush filled with native birds as the track crosses private farmland and the Hinewai Reserve and takes you along the spectacular coastline. The coastal area here is a marine mammal sanctuary, so you are likely to see penguins, seals and Hector's dolphins.

For bookings
PO Box 50, Akaroa
phone (03) 304 7612.

Shirley derive a lot of satisfaction from this. Currently they supplement local grapes with chardonnay from Marlborough but in the long term are looking to make wine entirely from Canterbury grapes.

The business hasn't stopped at wine production. Their property is only 15 minutes from the heart of Christchurch, and on the property there is a 120-year-old gatekeeper's lodge. This sits in a cottage garden surrounded by beautiful old trees. With some restoration it was ideal for a ready-made restaurant and sales area and has now become a very popular place to have lunch.

Shirley says that locals have been very supportive and they sell 50 percent of their wine production locally. Of course, the local market is also a finite market, so, using their experience in the beef trade, Brent and Shirley are now hoping to export their wines as well.

☛ **150 Old Tai Tapu Road, Christchurch**

Phone: (03) 322 7780

Fax: (03) 322 9273

Email: office@rossendale.co.nz

Hours: for tasting and buying wines, same as restaurant.

Eating/other facilities: restaurant open 10am-5pm daily and Thursday-Sunday evenings for dinner.

Owners: Brent and Shirley Rawstron

Winemaker: Grant Whelan

Wines produced

○ Rossendale Chardonnay, $14-16
Rossendale Barrel Selection Chardonnay, $18-20
Rossendale Gewürztraminer, $18-20
Rossendale Riesling, $12-13
Rossendale Sauvignon Blanc, $14-16

● Rossendale Pinot Noir, $16-18

St Helena Wine Estate _____

Established in 1978, this was the first commercial winery in Canterbury and it certainly made the New Zealand industry sit up when, in 1982, its pinot noir took gold at the National Wine Competition.

Robin Mundy and his brother Norman were the third generation in a family of vegetable growers, 80 percent of whose crop was potatoes. In the mid-1970s blight ruined the potato crops and they had to look for an alternative. They'd been looking into blackcurrants at Lincoln University (then Lincoln College) but got talking to Dr David Jackson about his viticultural trials. Then they started making history.

In the early days they sold all their wine in Canterbury. They now own a 21-hectare vineyard, and sell throughout New Zealand. Four years ago St Helena turned its attention to overseas markets, putting even more emphasis than before on their pinot noir. This pioneering vineyard has certainly been a success. As Robin says, 'It's been a learning curve! But the main difference is that when I went to meetings as a potato grower I could wear my Swanndri and boots. Now I often have to put on a suit.'

☛ **Coutts Island Road, Christchurch**

Phone: (03) 323 8202

Fax: (03) 323 8252

Hours: for tasting and buying wines, Monday-Saturday 10am-5pm, Sunday 12-5pm.

Eating/other facilities: none.

Owners: Robin and Bernice Mundy

Winemaker: Alan McCorkindale

Wines produced

○ St Helena Chardonnay, $15-17
St Helena Reserve Chardonnay, $25-28
St Helena Late Harvest Bacchus, $13-15

SKIING AND SNOW BOARDING

In winter the Southern Alps become a magnificent playground dotted with ski fields. The mid-Canterbury town of Methven, only an hour's drive from Christchurch in the rich farmland of the Canterbury Plains, is an ideal base for those who love mountain sports, being close to Mt Hutt and Porter Heights, the two commercial ski fields in the area. It's also a pretty good starting point for those who like salmon fishing and golf.

For Mt Hutt ski field phone (03) 302 8811 or (03) 308 5074.

For Porter Heights ski field phone (03) 379 7087.

AKAROA HARBOUR CRUISES

Main Wharf, Akaroa
freephone 0800 4 DOLPHINS
phone (03) 304 7641
fax (03) 304 7643

At Banks Peninsula it is possible to cruise out from the harbour of Akaroa where, as well as a wide variety of bird life, you can see the world's smallest dolphin, the Hector's dolphin.

ARTHUR'S PASS NATIONAL PARK

Situated in part of the Southern Alps mountain range, this area offers a variety of walks from short, easy strolls to demanding climbs. You can enjoy the beautiful forest, waterfalls, alpine gardens and stand on mountain tops with the most spectacular views. The park is administered by the Department of Conservation and they have an interesting visitor information centre with some fascinating historical displays.

See Information Centres for details.

St Helena Canterbury Plains Müller Thurgau, $7-8
St Helena Pinot Blanc, $12-14
St Helena Pinot Gris, $13-15
St Helena Reserve Pinot Gris, $22-24
St Helena Riesling, $10-12
St Helena Southern Alps Dry White, $7-8
St Helena Marlborough Sauvignon Blanc, $13-15

● St Helena Pinot Noir, $18-20
St Helena Port Hills Pinot Noir, $11-13
St Helena Reserve Pinot Noir, $28-32
St Helena Peers Port, $12-15

Sandihurst Wines

In 1999 John Brough of Sandihurst Wines took a gold medal and the trophy at the Royal Easter Show Wine Awards with his pinot noir. That's quite an achievement for a man who says he knew nothing about wine when he got started in the business.

He had been in the fishing industry, but in 1987 he left that and bought some land as an investment. Then he got into wine, and Sandihurst was established in 1992. John says that having lasted this long he reckons he'll survive! He likes the idea of staying small and being involved in the whole process – the growing, processing, and selling. John also believes that West Melton is one of the finest areas for growing pinot noir.

☞ **Main West Coast Road (Highway 73), West Melton**

Phone/fax: (03) 347 8289

Hours: for tasting and buying wines, 11am-4.30pm Saturday and Sunday. Other times can be arranged by appointment.

Eating/other facilities: none.

Owner: Sandihurst Wines Ltd

Winemaker: Alan McCorkindale

Wines produced

○ Sandihurst Chardonnay, $15-17
Sandihurst Gewürztraminer, $19-21
Sandihurst Pinot Gris, $19-21
Sandihurst Riesling, $15-17

● Sandihurst Pinot Noir, $28-32

Sherwood Estate Wines _____

Planting for this small estate vineyard began in 1987. Dayne Sherwood and his wife Jill had access to land 40 minutes' drive from Christchurch, and started with the intention of being both growers and winemakers. 'We always wanted to see the process through,' says Jill. They made their first wine in 1990. They've placed most emphasis on chardonnay and pinot noir, and have picked up many awards for the latter. Sherwood Estate has certainly established itself and now exports 80 percent of its wines.

Their restaurant, with both indoor and outdoor seating, is a delightful venue for lunch or dinner. This, too, came out of the pleasure of matching good wines with good food. And there is also a certain local pride: 'You don't have to go to Marlborough to enjoy something like this,' says Jill.

☞ **Cnr Weedons Ross Road & Johnson Road, West Melton**

Phone: (03) 347 9060

Fax: (03) 347 8225

Email: winery@sherwood.co.nz

Hours: for tasting and buying wines, same as restaurant.

HOT AIR BALLOONING

phone (03) 358 9859
fax (03) 358 9829
email: info@ballooning.co.nz

The Christchurch-based company Up, Up And Away was the first to establish ballooning in this region. It is a magnificent way to capture the Canterbury experience – fly in a balloon from the centre of the city and get a superb view of the Pacific Ocean, the Canterbury Plains and the Southern Alps. The best time of day to go ballooning is at dawn, so in optimum conditions you get to fly as the sun rises. Flying time is about one hour but passengers are encouraged to help in flight preparation – it all adds to the fun. After landing you can relax with a glass of bubbly. Launch sites are weather dependent, so the company informs passengers in good time before each flight.

BARRY'S BAY CHEESE

Main Road from Little River to Akaroa, Banks Peninsula
phone (03) 304 5809
fax (03) 304 5814

Among the hills on the way to Akaroa is Barry's Bay. There's not a lot there except the cheese factory! But it's well worth stopping and paying a visit. Not only is their range of cheeses very appealing, but every second day from October to April you can watch the cheese being made. Traditional cheese-making practices are used and it's fascinating to watch them being carried out. A great opportunity to buy some 'Barry's Bay Sharp' or 'Akaroa Mellow' to go with some local wine.

Eating/other facilities: restaurant open Wednesday-Sunday and public holidays, 11am-5pm; open late Friday and Saturday for dinner.

Owners: Dayne and Jill Sherwood

Winemaker: Dayne Sherwood

Wines produced

○   Sherwood Estate Chardonnay, $14-16
Sherwood Estate Reserve Chardonnay, $24-26
Sherwood Estate Single Vineyard Chardonnay, $19-22
Sherwood Estate Riesling, $14-16
Sherwood Estate Sauvignon Blanc, $14-16

●   Sherwood Estate Pinot Noir, $14-17
Sherwood Estate Reserve Pinot Noir, $24-27
Sherwood Estate Single Vineyard Pinot Noir, $19-22

Trent's Estate Vineyard _____

Just 20 minutes down the Main South Road from Christchurch, in pleasant rural countryside, is a 125-year-old triple-brick building that was originally a chicory drying kiln. It's now been converted into a delightful restaurant, serving tasty food in a casual atmosphere. Unusually, the building has below-ground fire pits and heating shafts – which means it's always warm at Trent's, even in mid-winter.

Relatively new to the scene, Trent's Estate Vineyard was established in 1995. They process their fruit at St Helena Wines, and released their first wines in 1999.

☞   **Trents Road, RD6, Christchurch**

Phone/fax: (03) 349 6940

Hours: for tasting and buying of wines, same as restaurant.

Darjon Vineyards, Canterbury

Langdale Wine Estate, Canterbury

Lake Wanaka, Central Otago

Chard Farm, Central Otago

Glowworm caves, Te Anau, Central Otago

Whitewater rafting, Shotover River, Central Otago

Bird and wasp protection,
Dry Gully Vineyard, Central Otago

Horse trekking, Walter Peak, Central Otago

Eating/other facilities: restaurant open Thursday-Sunday, 11am till late. The 95-seat restaurant (plus sheltered seating outside) provides light meals through to full dinners, and there are à la carte and blackboard menus.

Owners: John and Sue Shanks

Winemaker: Alan McCorkindale

Wines produced

○ Trent's Estate Chardonnay, $22-24
   Trent's Estate Riesling, $21-23

● Trent's Estate Pinot Noir, $26-29

TRANZALPINE EXPRESS

Regarded as one of the really great railway adventures anywhere in the world, this trip is a daily event between the east and west coasts of the South Island, leaving Christchurch at 8am. The train travels across the Canterbury Plains, through gorges and river valleys and into the Southern Alps – New Zealand's most spectacular mountain range. Then it plunges into the dramatically different landscape of the West Coast, descending through the beech forests to the coastal town of Greymouth. You can go all the way or you can disembark at Arthur's Pass, the alpine village that is a starting point for many wonderful bush walks. There is a return train each day, leaving Greymouth at 2.25pm.

For reservations and enquiries call freephone 0800 802 802.

central otago

REGIONAL HIGHLIGHTS

RIPPON ROCK FESTIVAL

An annual event held during Waitangi weekend, in early February, in the form of a summer day of music on the shores of Lake Wanaka.

For further information contact Lynne Christie through Rippon Vineyard phone (03) 443 8084.

OTAGO FOOD AND WINE FESTIVAL

Held over a weekend in early March, the festival takes place in Dunedin at Woodhaugh Gardens.

For further information contact Robert Bryson phone (03) 455 9934 or (025) 606 489.

WARBIRDS OVER WANAKA

Held at Easter every second year. This is a chance for buffs to see beautifully restored and much-loved old planes go through their paces. It's a great atmosphere.

For further information freephone 0800 4969 2000.

Central Otago is a dramatically beautiful area of New Zealand. It is much further inland than the other wine-making regions, and parts of it are very close to the stunning southern mountain ranges. These are the highest altitude vineyards in New Zealand. The region's climate is as dramatic as its scenery – hot, dry summers and cold winters.

This certainly isn't the easiest place in which to grow grapes. Frosts can be a real problem, threatening spring growth and the ripening fruit. On the other hand, this southern region has many hours of summer sunlight, which means the fruit gets to ripen over a long period. The autumns may be short but they're dry, allowing the fruit to be left for late picking. And both viticulturists and winegrowers are excited by Central's unique growing conditions – it's the only place in the country where grapes are grown in a continental climate.

There were winemaking ventures in Central Otago as far back as the 1860s, when the area was more famous for its goldfields. A French goldminer, Jean Desire Feraud, came to Otago in the goldrush of 1862. He saw the potential of the area and for the next 20 years made a variety of wines, some of which won prizes in Sydney wine competitions. His original stone winery, near the town of Clyde, stands today. But, like the gold, viticulture all but disappeared. That was until the 1970s. The first commercially produced wine was released in 1987.

By the 1990s Central Otago pinot noir and chardonnay were making a fine name for themselves and some very interesting riesling, gewürztraminer and sauvignon blanc were coming out of the region. Wine lovers were starting to talk of Rippon, Chard Farm, Gibbston Valley, Taramea and Black Ridge. Now, Central Otago is the fastest-growing wine region in New Zealand,

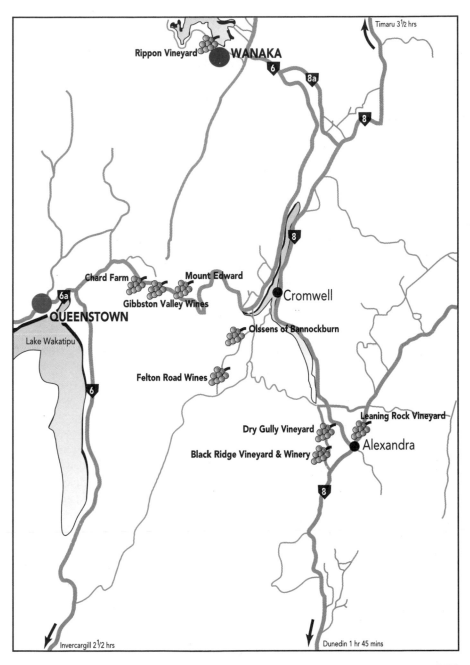

Timaru 3½ hrs

Rippon Vineyard · WANAKA

6

8a

8

8

Chard Farm · Mount Edward

Gibbston Valley Wines

6a · Cromwell

QUEENSTOWN

Lake Wakatipu · Olssens of Bannockburn

6 · Felton Road Wines

Leaning Rock Vineyard

Dry Gully Vineyard

Black Ridge Vineyard & Winery · Alexandra

8

Invercargill 2½ hrs

Dunedin 1 hr 45 mins

REGIONAL HIGHLIGHTS

QUEENSTOWN WINTER FESTIVAL

Held in the third week of July, events take place at two of the terrific skifields in the area – Coronet Peak and The Remarkables – and in downtown Queenstown. There's crazy creativity in the Birdman Pier Jump for those who fancy they can fly and the Peak to Peak race for those who know they can ski!

For further information phone (03) 442 4620.

QUEENSTOWN SPRING CARNIVAL

Mid-September silliness! Held on The Remarkables ski area with 'silly races' and the Extreme Skiing competition. All great fun.

For further information phone (03) 442 4620.

and since 1990 Central Otago pinot noir has topped its class five times in national wine competitions.

The region also has plenty of other things to attract visitors. In winter the mountains offer wonderful skiing for anyone from beginners to downhill slalom racers. From the tops of these skifields you get breathtaking views of mountain range upon mountain range – small wonder they are named The Remarkables. Add to this the beautiful valleys and lakes and you're not far short of paradise! And paradise with plenty of activities on offer, not the least being wine cellar tours organised by Gibbston Valley Wines. A little further afield from Queenstown and Wanaka, but well worth a visit in its own right, is the town of Te Anau, the gateway to the Milford Sound. Taking a boat cruise around the sound and to the underwater observatory is a must. Whilst in Te Anau, don't miss the opportunity to see the attractions there, such as the muted magnificence of the underground glow-worm caves.

Lake Wanaka, surrounded by mountains, provides great summer fun as well. At its heart is Mount Aspiring National Park, which offers wonderful climbing or tramping adventures. The lake itself is ideal for water-skiing and boating. There are plenty of good rivers in the area for anglers and, if pumping adrenalin is your thing, this is the home of bungy jumping. Leap into the void over the Kawarau Gorge or off Skippers Bridge. Another buzz for thrill seekers is to go jet-boating or whitewater rafting on the Shotover River, through the steep-sided gorges of the area. If you prefer to remain rather more closely fixed to the earth, try your luck at the centuries-old art of gold-panning. Or, just enjoy the outstanding scenery from on board the vintage steamship TSS *Earnslaw* as she cruises around Lake Wakatipu.

Alexandra
22 Centennial Avenue
PO Box 56
phone (03) 448 9515
fax (03) 440 2061
email: alvin@nzhost.co.nz

Cromwell
47 The Mall
PO Box 2
phone (03) 445 0212
fax (03) 445 1319
email: crovin@nzhost.co.nz

Queenstown
Clock Tower Building
Cnr. Shotover and Camp Streets
PO Box 253
phone (03) 442 4100
fax (03) 442 8907
email: qvc@xtra.co.nz

Te Anau
Lake Front Drive
PO Box 1
phone (03) 249 8900
fax (03) 249 7022
email: teuvin@nzhost.co.nz

Wanaka
DOC Building
Cnr Ballantyne Street
PO Box 147
phone (03) 443 1233
fax (03) 443 1290

AUTHOR'S FAVOURITES

Black Ridge Pinot Noir

Chard Farm Judge & Jury Chardonnay

Chard Farm Gewürztraminer

Gibbston Valley Pinot Noir

Rippon Pinot Noir

the wineries

Black Ridge Vineyard ————

This is the most southern winery in the world. And it must have one of the most dramatic settings. Black Ridge is a wild and rocky place with schist rock outcrops dominating the vineyard. It's been described as 'primeval' and is certainly worth a visit just to admire the courage of anyone setting out to turn it into a vineyard. This was once a thriving gold mining area but is now home to one of Central Otago's pioneering vineyards. There are 7.5 hectares planted in grapes and, as they say, where grapes can't be planted the rocks are left to the wild thyme and the rabbits. Sue Edwards and Verdun Burgess established Black Ridge Vineyard in 1981 and produced their first wines – a riesling and a gewürztraminer – in 1988. Since then they've gained a reputation for excellent quality wines. Their pinot noir in particular has been a pretty consistent gold medal winner and their chardonnay, riesling and gewürztraminer have also won awards.

☞ **Conroys Road, 6 km from Alexandra, Central Otago**
Phone: (03) 449 2059

CAPRICCIO'S RESTAURANT & BAR

Pembroke Mall, Wanaka
phone/fax (03) 433 8579

The restaurant is above a bank on the lakefront in Wanaka. Like many in the area, it makes the most of New Zealand's succulent lamb, venison and seafood. It also specialises in pasta dishes. Fully licensed, it is open daily from 6pm until late.

Fax: (03) 449 2597

Email: blkridge@es.co.nz

Hours: 10am-5pm daily.

Eating/other facilities: none.

Owners: Sue Edwards and Verdun Burgess

Winemaker: Tim Wardwell

Wines produced

○ Black Ridge Chardonnay, $19-22
Black Ridge Gewürztraminer, $16-19
Black Ridge Otago Gold, $12-14
Black Ridge Riesling (dry and medium), $16-18

● Black Ridge Cabernet Sauvignon, $19-22
Black Ridge Pinot Noir, $29-34

Chard Farm

It's a steep, narrow climb to this beautiful vineyard 70 metres above the Kawarau River and 20 kilometres from Queenstown. In fact, it's not far from the Kawarau Bridge, which is used these days for bungy jumping. It's worth the journey to Chard Farm for its excellent wines, as well as the great views. This is another property that has strong historical links with the gold rush of the late 1800s. Richard Chard established a market garden here to supply the miners. And Chard Road was once part of the main coach link between Cromwell and Queenstown.

The vineyard was started in 1986 by Rob and Greg Hay. Rob had spent three years in Germany learning the art of winemaking. It's a commonly held view in Europe that great wine is made in a challenging environment. The Hay brothers certainly picked one, with huge rocky outcrops plunging down to the Kawarau Gorge. Look for the 'Judge and Jury', an amazing rock formation that

CARDRONA HOTEL

Cardrona (at the foot of the skifield and a 15 minute drive from Wanaka)
phone (03) 443 8153

This is an historic building and, with its very rustic atmosphere and piano in the corner, it's easy to feel as if you've stepped back in time. The bar and restaurant meals include great local produce like venison and salmon. The hotel is fully licensed and BYO. It's closed from the second week in May to 15 June. Otherwise it's open daily from 11am until late.

THE COLONEL'S HOMESTEAD

Walter Peak, Steamer Wharf, Queenstown
phone (03) 442 7500

This contact number is for booking a cruise on the TSS *Earnslaw*, which you must take to reach the Colonel's Homestead Restaurant on the waterfront of the historic Walter Peak High Country Station. Have a barbecue meal on the terraces or enjoy something from the carvery inside. The cruises run from 6pm daily from October to mid-April.

CORONATION BATHHOUSE CAFÉ AND RESTAURANT

Marine Parade, Queenstown
phone (03) 442 5625

Right on the beach, this original Victorian bathhouse was built in 1911. It's been turned into a haven of freshly baked pastries and terrific coffee during the day. The restaurant offers fine dining with gourmet local produce in the evening. It's fully licensed. Open from 10am until late, Tuesday-Sunday. Closed on Mondays.

NUGGET POINT RESTAURANT

Nugget Point Resort, Arthur's Point, Queenstown
phone (03) 442 7273

A New Zealand Tourism Award winner in 1998 and previously granted the New Zealand Beef and Lamb Hallmark of Excellence, Nugget Point Restaurant offers 'traditional dishes combined with the distinctive tastes of New Zealand' as well as an extensive vegetarian menu. Open daily from 6pm to 9pm. Reservations are recommended.

overlooks the vineyard and after which is named the winery's top-of-the-line chardonnay.

A tasting session at Chard Farm is always informative and frequently very good fun. (Did I really mean to buy six bottles of the Judge & Jury Chardonnay!) Chard Farm has also gone into a joint venture to establish a 'House of Méthode Champenoise' at their Lake Hayes vineyard. In 1999 they had their first release under the name of Perrelle Lake Hayes.

☞ **Chard Road, off State Highway 1, Central Otago**

Phone: (03) 442 6110

Fax: (03) 441 8400

Email: chardfarm@xtra.co.nz

Hours: 10am-5pm, seven days.

Eating/other facilities: none.

Owners: Rob Hay and Gerda Schumann

Winemakers: Rob Hay and Duncan Forsyth

Wines produced

○ Chard Farm Judge & Jury Chardonnay, $29-33
Chard Farm Closeburn Chardonnay, $19-22
Chard Farm Gewürztraminer, $19-22
Chard Farm Pinot Gris, $21-24
Chard Farm Riesling, $18-20
Chard Farm Rosé, $13-15
Chard Farm Sauvignon Blanc, $18-20

● Chard Farm Bragato Reserve Pinot Noir, $39-45
Chard Farm Finla Mor Pinot Noir, $27-30
Chard Farm River Run Pinot Noir, $21-24

Dry Gully Vineyard

Dry Gully is a boutique vineyard, hand-tended by Sibylla and Bill Moffitt and their family. This was once an area rich in gold but, when Bill and Sibylla bought the property in the late 1970s, it was an apricot orchard. The trees were over one hundred years old and not producing well, so in 1992 the Moffitts decided to plant vines.

Their other decision was to specialise in pinot noir. They wanted to focus on producing a really top quality wine. Their first vintage was produced in 1997 and went on to win a gold medal at the 1998 Liquorland Royal Easter Show. It was also recognised for its high quality in being awarded the title of 'Best Red Wine in the High Priced Category'. Plans to retire and have time for whitebaiting and travelling around the country in summer have had to be put on hold! It was an excellent beginning and Dry Gully continues to produce some special pinot noirs.

☛ **Earnscleugh Road, Alexandra, Central Otago**
Phone/fax: (03) 449 2030
Hours: for tasting and purchasing, by appointment.
Eating/other facilities: none.
Owners: Bill and Sibylla Moffitt
Winemakers: Rudi Bauer and Dean Shaw

Wine produced
● Dry Gully Pinot Noir, $25-30

Felton Road Wines

Established in 1991, Felton Road was one of the newer wineries in Central Otago, causing a lot of excitement in 1997 with the release of their first vintage. Their Block Three Pinot Noir was so well regarded that it sold out almost immediately, and it was a similar story with the

RELISHES CAFÉ

1/99 Ardmore Street, Wanaka
phone (03) 443 9018

This popular café opposite the wharf in Wanaka is open for breakfast, lunch and dinner. It's wise to make a booking, especially for dinner. It has a blackboard menu featuring beautifully cooked, interesting dishes. Relishes is fully licensed but it also has a BYO licence. Open daily 9am-3pm for breakfast and lunch and from 6pm for dinner.

ROARING MEG'S

57 Shotover Street, Queenstown
phone (03) 442 9676

This atmospheric restaurant's got history! It is named after one of the two notorious 'ladies' who brought comfort to the goldminers of the late 1800s. The house was originally built in Skipper's Canyon, but was brought to Queenstown on horse-drawn carts in 1922. Fifty years later it became Roaring Meg's. It's fully licensed with an extensive wine list. Open daily from 6.30pm.

FERRY HOTEL GUESTHOUSE

*Spence Road, Lower
Shotover, Queenstown
phone (03) 442 2194
fax (03) 442 2190
email: ferry@clear.net.nz*

$$-$$$

This historic hotel was originally a resting place for travellers waiting to cross the Shotover River by ferry. Now the 1872 heritage-listed building has been extensively renovated. There are three guest bedrooms and a lounge with a log burner to make it cosy in winter. In summer guests can make use of the cottage garden and the barbecue.

regular pinot noir. It comes as no surprise that subsequently they have been awarded trophies for this wine. Felton Road white wines have also all been awarded medals. Just eight kilometres from Cromwell, the three-level winery is built into the hillside with an underground barrel cellar. Like many in the area, the winery has very attractive vineyards and impressive mountain views.

☞ **Felton Road, Bannockburn, Central Otago**

Phone: (03) 445 0885

Fax: (03) 445 0881

Email: feltonrdwines@xtra.co.nz

Hours: 10am-5pm seven days; closed weekends May-October.

Eating/other facilities: none.

Owners: Felton Road Wines Ltd

Winemaker: Blair Walter

Wines produced

○ Felton Road Chardonnay, $22-24
Felton Road Chardonnay Barrel Fermented, $30-33
Felton Road Riesling, $19-21
Felton Road Dry Riesling, $19-21
Felton Road Riesling Block One, $24-26
Felton Road Sauvignon Blanc, $19-21
Felton Road Vin Gris, $19-21

● Felton Road Pinot Noir, $36-40
Felton Road Pinot Noir Block Three, $46-50

Gibbston Valley Wines _____

Alan Brady was the pioneer in this, Central Otago's first commercial winery, which was established in 1983. It is the largest producer in the region. When Gibbston Valley became a 300-tonne winery Alan decided it was time to move on to his new venture at Mount Edward and to concentrate on his passion for pinot noir. But that's another story (see Mount Edward winery).

Gibbston Valley, a 20-minute drive from Queenstown, lies at the foot of the rocky bluffs of the Kawarau Gorge. Among its many attractions is New Zealand's largest wine cellar, tunnelled 76 metres underground into the rock hillside. It's kept at a constant temperature (around 14 degrees Celsius) and provides a 'perfect haven' for the maturation of the pinot noir and chardonnay. It also adds something special to one's wine tasting experience. The winery's first vintage was bottled in 1984 and Gibbston Valley Pinot Noir has subsequently stood out. But their other wines have also had much success at national wine competitions. The wines made from estate-grown grapes are labelled 'Estate Reserve' and those made from fruit brought in from other regions are always clearly labelled.

Gibbston Valley also offers an excellent restaurant that is open from 10 in the morning to late afternoon. Oysters in season, smoked salmon, venison, scrumptious platters with award-winning cheeses...what better way to finish up a wine cellar tour?

OLIVERS LODGE AND RESTAURANT

34 Sunderland Street, Clyde
phone (03) 449 2860
fax (03) 449 2862

$$-$$$

This lovely place is steeped in history. Built in the late 1800s as a general store, the original buildings consisted of the storefront, stables, homestead, barn, servants' quarters and smokehouse – all constructed from the local schist rock. Keeping the original walls and weather-beaten timbers, Olivers has turned them into a superb lodge with 12 ensuite guest rooms. The setting is just as charming with extensive English-style gardens.

☞ **Gibbston, Main Queenstown-Cromwell Highway, Central Otago**

Phone: (03) 442 6910

Fax: (03) 442 6909

Email: ross@gibbstonvalleywines.co.nz

Website: www.gibbston-valley-wines.co.nz

Hours: for tasting and purchasing, 10am-5.30pm daily. Wine cave tour and tasting on the hour 10am-4pm.

Eating/other facilities: restaurant open daily 10 am-3pm, evenings by arrangement.

Owners: shareholders

Winemaker: Grant Taylor

REMARKABLES LODGE

State Highway 6,
Queenstown
phone/fax (03) 442 2720

$$$

In 1997 this lodge was voted 'Boutique Hotel of the Year' in the New Zealand Tourism Awards. With its own helipad, the lodge is sited at the foot of the Remarkables and offers complete luxury only minutes from the skifield access road. An outdoor hot tub, a solar-heated swimming pool, a tennis court, an in-house restaurant and a library enhance the elegant accommodation.

THE STONE COTTAGE

Dublin Bay, Wanaka
phone (03) 443 1878
fax (03) 443 1276

$$$

The loft of The Stone Cottage has two self-contained suites with private balconies. The breathtaking view sweeps from Lake Wanaka to the Treble Cone skifield. The cottage was built in 1977 using local schist and is set in a lakeside garden. All suites have an

Wines produced

○ Gibbston Valley Chardonnay, $25-29
Gibbston Valley Greenstone (Chardonnay), $19-22
Gibbston Valley Pinot Gris, $20-22
Gibbston Valley Riesling, $19-21
Gibbston Valley Sauvignon Blanc (Marlborough) $18-21
Gibbston Valley Sauvignon Blanc (Central Otago), $18-20

● Gibbston Valley Pinot Noir, $29-32
Gibbston Valley Reserve Pinot Noir, $48-54
Gibbston Valley Gold River (Pinot Noir), $19-22

Leaning Rock Vineyard _____

Dhana Pillai and Mark Hesson come from the Otago area. Both were qualified geologists metal detecting for gold in Western Australia at a time when the wine industry there was expanding. Both of them were struck by the same thought: 'We could do this! It's a good excuse to work on the land, which we love.' They returned to New Zealand and, with some expert advice, looked at a number of sites between Roxburgh and Wanaka before settling on their present property near Alexandra. It provides excellent shelter and suitable soil. And in 1995 they crushed their first grapes.

☛ **188 Hillview Road, Alexandra, Central Otago**

Phone/fax: (03) 448 9169

Email: dhanap@es.co.nz

Hours: for tasting and purchasing, by appointment.

Eating/other facilities: none.

Owners/winemakers: Mark Hesson and Dhana Pillai

Wines produced

○ Leaning Rock Chardonnay, $28-32
   Leaning Rock Gewürztraminer, $18-21
   Leaning Rock Riesling, $18-20

● Leaning Rock Pinot Noir, $28-33

Mount Edward _____

Alan Brady had an eye for the commercial production of wine in this southern region and was a pioneer in making it happen. He'd come to New Zealand from Ireland when he was 23 years old. He worked as a newspaper journalist, including spending time on the *Otago Daily Times*. Television then beckoned and Alan worked in Dunedin as a news editor. His next move was to go freelance.

But in 1976 Alan bought some land at Gibbston Valley. Five years later he planted grapes, his first vintage was bottled in 1984 and the region's largest winery was launched.

After Gibbston Valley's initial success, Alan decided to focus on pinot noir. He established Mount Edward and, with a bit of help from winemaker Grant Taylor, is virtually a one-man-band from growing, to processing, to selling his wine. He grows and produces a little riesling as well, but it is the pinot noir that is his passion.

☞ **Coalpit Road, Gibbston, Central Otago**

   Phone: (03) 442 6113

   Fax: (03) 442 9119

   Email: abrady@queenstown.co.nz

   Hours: for tasting and purchasing, by appointment.

   Eating/other facilities: none.

   Owner: Alan Brady

   Winemakers: Alan Brady and Grant Taylor

(cont'd)
external staircase and a kitchen with breakfast ingredients and basics is provided. It's only 10 minutes' drive from Wanaka but if you want to eat in, you can dine with your host downstairs.

TE WANAKA LODGE

23 Brownston Street, Wanaka
phone (03) 443 9224
fax (03) 443 9246
freephone 0800 WANAKA,
email: tewanakalodge@xtra.
co.nz

$$-$$$

This chalet was purpose-built as a B&B facility in the heart of Wanaka. It's very comfortable – all the rooms have a private balcony but there are two guest lounges if you're feeling sociable. Each has a log fire for warming up after a day in the snow. Or you can relax in a cedar hot tub. The tariff includes a gourmet breakfast.

TRELAWN PLACE

Gorge Road, Arthur's Point,
Queenstown
phone/fax (03) 442 9160

$$$

The historic and the new combine happily on this property. The romantic stone cottage dates back to the goldrush days when it was a miner's hut. It's the perfect place for a honeymoon. Trelawn itself was built in the mid-1980s. It has a distant mountain view but is sited above the Shotover River, with its gardens and lawns sweeping to the cliff edge.

Wines produced

○ Mount Edward Riesling, $18-20

● Mount Edward Pinot Noir, $33-38

Olssens of Bannockburn _____

Established in 1989, this is a garden vineyard with five hectares of rural and landscaped grounds. Thousands of bulbs have been planted, along with 7500 trees and shrubs. And although John Olssen and Heather Forsyth have recently opened a café, visitors are still welcome to bring a picnic and relax in this beautiful environment. The hills of Bannockburn are covered in thyme and the vines are deeply rooted in the rocky soils. Olssens has supplied grapes to Chard Farm for three years, but 1997 saw the first wines released under their own label.

☞ **306 Felton Road, Bannockburn, Central Otago**

Phone: (03) 445 1716

Fax: (03) 445 0050

Email: olssenj@xtra.co.nz

Hours: for tasting and purchasing, daily 10am-4pm October-May. Closed weekends May-October but will open by appointment.

Eating/other facilities: café open for snacks and lunches. Visitors can also bring a picnic lunch.

Owners: John Olssen and Heather Forsyth

Winemaker: Duncan Forsyth

Wines produced

○ Olssens of Bannockburn Chardonnay, $23-28
Olssens of Bannockburn Gewürztraminer, $19-22
Olssens of Bannockburn Riesling, $18-20
Olssens of Bannockburn Sauvignon Blanc, $18-21

● Olssens of Bannockburn Pinot Noir, $28-32
 Flapjack Creek Reserve Pinot Noir, $37-42

Rippon Vineyard

Rolfe and Lois Mills believe theirs is New Zealand's highest vineyard. It must surely be one of the world's most beautiful. From the winery up on the rise you can look down over the vineyard, which is planted on the schist slopes dropping towards Lake Wanaka. Looking over the vines and across the waters, you have a magnificent view of the imposing Buchanan Range at the head of the lake.

It all began in 1976, early days for wine growing in this region. Rolfe had been South Island manager for the Dunedin-based family business. The family also owned Wanaka Station, which presented an opportunity when Rolfe was looking for a career change. That year Rolfe and Lois began planting the vines. In 1981 they went to Bergerac, in the south-west of France, to learn more about the art of growing grapes, and returned to complete the establishment of the vineyard in 1986. Rippon now has a reputation for excellent wines. Their best known is the pinot noir, which is regarded as a classic wine. The 'Emma Rippon' is their méthode champenoise, named for Rolfe's great-great-grandmother. Rippon has a Bio Gro certification for organic wines.

☞ **Mt Aspiring Road, Lake Wanaka, Central Otago**

 Phone: (03) 443 8084

 Fax: (03) 443 8034

 Email: rippon@xtra.co.nz

 Website: www.rippon.co.nz

 Hours: for tasting and purchasing, December-May 11am-5pm, July-November 1pm-4.30pm Closed May-June (open by appointment only).

VILLA SORGENFREI

11 Lake Hayes Road, Lake Hayes, Queenstown
phone (03) 442 1128
fax (03) 442 1239
freephone 0800 271 128

$$$

Coronet Peak and The Remarkables provide the mountain views from this lakeside villa. 'Sorgenfrei' is German for 'worry-free', and the villa certainly has a wonderfully relaxing atmosphere. Its stone walls, shingle roof, slate floors, kauri ceilings and exposed beams are all the features of homes in Otago's colonial past. But this is a modern home, built in 1989, so you get the best of both eras! The guest rooms are upstairs, but meals are taken either in the dining room or on the terrace.

WILLOW COTTAGE

Maxwell Road, Mount Barker, Wanaka
phone/fax (03) 443 8856

$$-$$$

This is a delightful country stay only five minutes' drive away from Wanaka township. It's an original farm homestead cob cottage built in 1875. There's nothing old-fashioned about the comfort in the cottage but the furniture is genuine colonial. Willow Cottage is quite separate from the homestead and you can either cook your own breakfast or have it cooked for you, there or over at the homestead.

Eating/other facilities: gourmet vineyard lunches served, and a special Christmas lunch.

Owners: Rolfe and Lois Mills

Winemaker: Russell Lake

Wines produced

○ Rippon Chardonnay, $24-27
Emma Rippon (bottle fermented champenoise), $54-60
Rippon Gewürztraminer, $19-22
Rippon Hotere White, $13-15
Rippon Osteiner, $15-17
Rippon Riesling, $21-24
Rippon Gamay Rosé, $15-17
Rippon Sauvignon Blanc, $22-25

● Rippon Merlot Syrah, $28-32
Rippon Pinot Noir, $35-40

ARROWTOWN

This delightful little town is a very popular visitor destination. It was full of bustle and business in the goldrush days. Take a picnic, hire a gold pan and try your luck in the shallows of the Arrow River. The Lake District's Centennial Museum in Buckingham Street is an excellent place to go for local history, and a short stroll beside the river will bring you to the restored Chinese Miners' Village. Arrowtown is famous throughout the country for its autumn colours, as the English deciduous trees lining the main road display their magnificent palette of golds, reds and ambers.

JET BOATING

Thrills through the Shotover River Canyon or on the rugged Dart River can be had from Queenstown and up the Clutha River from Wanaka. It's breath-catching stuff. There are a number of companies that provide these trips. The Information Centres in each area are excellent places to get details.

FISHING

Try your luck fishing off a boat on Lake Wakatipu or from the banks of several local rivers. Quinnat salmon and brown and rainbow trout provide the challenge.

Good contacts are:
Fishing and Hunting Services
phone/fax (03) 443 9257
email: gtelfor@es.co.nz

A Fly Fishers Guide
44 Russell Street, Wanaka
phone (03) 443 7870
fax (03) 443 7853.

SKIING

Central Otago offers wonderful winter sports. Skiing is usually available between June and October. There are four major commercial fields in the area: Coronet Peak, Cardrona, The Remarkables and Treble Cone. They all offer downhill skiing on beginners slopes, as well as routes for the very experienced. The scenery is magnificent and the facilities are excellent. There are also telemark and cross-country skiing options. Or experience the thrill of heli-skiing – make your mark across untracked powder slopes in areas where the only access is by helicopter.

RIVER KAYAKING

Alpine River Guides
PO Box 9, Wanaka
phone/fax (03) 443 9023
An excellent way to enjoy this fascinating countryside, especially if you take a guided trip through the deep pools and rapids of the local rivers. With tuition, transport, equipment and food included, you can't help but enjoy the experience.

BUNGY JUMPING

This is real thrill-seeker territory and a Queenstown speciality. The original AJ Hackett jump in Central Otago was off the Kawarau Bridge – give it a go, or try '71 metres of wild gravity' at Skippers Canyon Suspension Bridge. Also at Skippers Canyon is the 'Pipeline' Bungy where you can terrify yourself with a 102-metre leap from the bridge.

Contacts
AJ Hackett Bungy, bookings at The Station, Cnr Camp and Shotover Streets, Queenstown
phone (03) 442 7100

The Pipeline HQ
27 Shotover Street, Queenstown
phone (03) 442 5455
fax (03) 442 4029

WALKING

The other great drawcard of this region is the opportunity it offers for exceptional walks through some of the most spectacular countryside in the world. At the heart of the Wanaka region is Mt Aspiring National Park, where you can explore mountains, lakes and rivers and enjoy the peace and grandeur of New Zealand's native bush. Queenstown is the starting point for some of New Zealand's most famous and popular walks – the Milford Track, the Routeburn and the Greenstone. Each of the towns in the area also has shorter and less demanding walks that are just as pleasurable. Regardless of whether you are attempting a long tramp or just a short hike, it is important to be properly equipped and familiar with details of track and weather conditions. Some longer hikes and guided tramping trips require you to book ahead to ensure placement and accommodation in the huts. There's a tremendous wealth of information available about the walks, and information centres can supply details, maps, etc.

SCENIC FLIGHTS

This stunning area encompasses mountains, glaciers and bush-clad valleys. Take them all in from the air and even fly to Milford Sound to meet up with the launch that can take you on your next adventure.

Contact
Aspiring Air at Wanaka Airport
PO Box 68, Wanaka
phone (03) 443 7943
fax (03) 443 8949
freephone 0800 100 943

TSS EARNSLAW

Phone (03) 442 7500

At a rather more sedate pace this elegant old steamship cruises Lake Wakatipu from August to May. Take a trip over to Walter Peak, the famous high country sheep station. Visit the homestead, enjoy the gardens and have a barbecue on the terraces overlooking the lake.

HORSE TREKKING

This is a very popular activity; you can either ride around local farms or into the countryside. Again, there are quite a number of companies who offer treks, suitable both for beginners and experienced riders.

For details contact the local information centres.

index of wineries

tasting notes

tasting notes